Contents

ACKNOWLEDGEMENTS

In 1997, the Social Work Research Centre of the University of Stirling organised an international conference entitled "On the Margins: Social Exclusion and Social Work", to explore the implications of social exclusion for social work. The conference attracted academics, policy makers, users and practitioners working within a wide range of disciplines in over 20 countries world-wide. We would like to extend our thanks not only to the original presenters of the keynote papers at that conference who have been kind enough to adapt their contributions for this book, but also to the authors of the concluding chapter.

We are equally grateful to the following people for their support, advice and patience during the compilation of this book. The practical help in producing and editing this book has been invaluable, not least from Jon Best, Alison Bowes, Sheena Conroy, Pam Lavery, Cherry Rowlings and Roger Sidaway. At the end of the day, this publication would not have been possible without the encouragement of Geoffrey Mann and his colleagues at Russell House Publishing Ltd, and we would also like to thank them for their support.

Monica Barry
Christine Hallett   August, 1998

i

LIST OF CONTRIBUTORS

Monica Barry is a Research Fellow in the Social Work Research Centre of the University of Stirling where she has worked since 1994. During this time, she has been involved in a joint evaluation of social work and criminal justice undertaken by the Social Work Research Centre in collaboration with The Scottish Office and a study of young people and crime. Prior to joining the Centre, she worked as a social worker in the voluntary sector. Her research interests include young people and social exclusion, offending and empowerment.

Peter Beresford works with Open Services Project, is Reader in Social Policy at Brunel University and a member of Survivors Speak Out, the national organisation and network of psychiatric system survivors. Recent publications include *It's Our Welfare: Report of the Citizen's Commission on the Future of the Welfare State* (1997, NISW) and *Poverty First Hand (1998, CPAG)*.

Juliet Cheetham has worked as a practitioner, teacher and researcher of social work. In 1986 she became the first Director of the Social Work Research Centre at the University of Stirling and was appointed Professor Emeritus in 1995. She has published widely on the evaluation of social work and on social work, ethnicity and race relations. Recently she extended her career beyond the confines of conventional academic life, directing a project for the Scottish Higher Education Funding Council to promote the interests of contract researchers, developing local authority community care practice and informing the research activities of a health care trust.

Navnit Dholakia is a member of the House of Lords with responsibility for the Home Office and European social policy, having recently left the Police Complaints Authority. Prior to that, he was the Head of Administration of Justice Section at the Commission for Racial Equality. He has served as a Senior Magistrate, is Vice-Chairman of the National Association for the Care and Resettlement of Offenders (NACRO), is on the Councils of Save the Children Fund and the Howard League for Penal Reform, and on the Community Services Development Committee of the Mental Health Foundation.

Bill Fisher has been an activist in the disability movement for 12 years. He is a founder member of The Lothian Coalition of Disabled People, Freespace Housing, Lothian Centre for Integrated Living and Access Ability Lothian, and from 1989-92 was General Secretary of the British Council of Organisations of Disabled People. Bill is a member of the Board of Management of Horizon Housing Association and Council Member of the Scottish Federation of Housing Associations, encouraging these organisations to promote good practice in the provision of housing for disabled people.

Roger Fuller is Deputy Director of the Social Work Research Centre, University of Stirling, where he has been working since its inception in 1986. He has been a researcher in social policy and social work since the early 1970s, and has experience of working in universities, local authorities and the voluntary sector. He has particular interests in methods of evaluating social work, social work with children and young people, and practitioner research.

Christine Hallett is Professor of Social Policy, Director of the Social Work Research Centre and Head of the Department of Applied Social Science at the University of Stirling. Her research interests include child welfare, juvenile justice and gender and social policy. Her publications include *Women and Social Policy* (ed.) (1996) and several books and articles on aspects of child abuse and child welfare policy.

Mary Hartnoll has worked in Social Work in Scotland since 1978 when she became Director of Social Work for Grampian Region. In 1993 she became Director of Social Work in Scotland's largest region, Strathclyde, prior to taking over as Director of Social Work for Glasgow City Council following local authority re-organisation in 1995. She is a member of the Consultative Committee on Social Work in the criminal justice field, Convenor of the Children and Families Committee of the Association of Directors of Social Work (of which she was previously President and Secretary) and was until recently a member of the Child Care Law Review for Scotland.

Bob Holman was a child care officer before entering academic life where he became Professor of Social Policy at the University of Bath. He has spent the last 21 years working with neighbourhood projects on council estates, and is also Visiting Professor at the Centre for the Child and Society, University of Glasgow. His recent books include *FARE Dealing: Neighbourhood Involvement in a Housing Scheme* (Community Development Foundation) and *Towards Equality* (SPCK). His new book, *Faith in the Poor*, will be published by Lion Publishing in August 1998.

Ruth Lister is Professor of Social Policy at Loughborough University. She is a former Director of the Child Poverty Action Group and sat on the Commission on Social Justice. She has published widely on issues around poverty, income maintenance and citizenship. Her most recent book, *Citizenship: Feminist Perspectives*, was published by Macmillan in 1997.

David Smith has been Professor of Social Work at Lancaster University since 1993. He qualified as a social worker at Exeter University and worked for four years as a probation officer before moving to Lancaster University in 1976. He has researched and published on a range of topics in social work and criminal justice, including crime prevention, inter-agency co-operation and victim-offender mediation. He is currently evaluating projects for persistent juvenile offenders and victim witnesses for The Scottish Office and working on an ESRC-funded project on racial violence in Greater Manchester.

Fiona Williams is Professor of Social Policy in the Department of Sociology and Social Policy at the University of Leeds. She has written widely on social divisions and social welfare. She is most well-known as the author of *Social Policy, A Critical Introduction: Issues of 'Race', Gender and Class* (1989, Polity Press) but she has also written on community care, learning disability, masculinities and postmodernism. Her current research interests are in comparative social policy, social movements and the restructuring of welfare.

Anne Wilson is a psychiatric system survivor. She works part-time as a social work tutor. In order to protect her identity she is using a pseudonym.

Gail Wilson is Senior Lecturer in Social Policy and Ageing at the Department of Social Policy and Administration, London School of Economics. She has worked on the distribution of resources within households, the lifestyles of older men and women and the delivery and evaluation of health and social services for older people. She is editor of *Community Care: Asking the Users* (1995, Chapman and Hall) as well as other publications on ageing and social theory.

PREFACE

This is a timely book, reflecting increased political interest in the topic of social exclusion. It explores the nature and processes of social exclusion and considers the ways and extent to which social work services impact upon the excluded. For some years now, the term social exclusion has been deployed with respect to the social policies of the European Union. In practice, however, despite the many and varied meanings of the term which are discussed in this book, in the context of the European Union social exclusion has been defined rather narrowly, principally referring to exclusion from the labour market. The different forms of social exclusion which may arise in other ways, for example as a result of disability, old age, minority ethnic status or gender, have received less attention in European social policy. The term social exclusion is now increasingly used in respect of social policies in the UK. A dynamic emphasis on the multiple processes of social exclusion and their impact on the lives and life courses of different social groups has, to some extent, replaced the traditional concern of social policy analysts with poverty. The current emphasis is on social exclusion as a relational process which includes both the 'included' and the 'excluded'. Whatever its long-term practical and policy outcomes may prove to be, the Social Exclusion Unit established by the New Labour government in 1997 is testament to the salience of the topic.

Accompanying an emphasis on social exclusion is the promotion of policies of social inclusion. Among these, social work, operating as it does with the disadvantaged and those on the margins of society, has an important role to play. While it is not to be expected that social work services alone can remedy the structural disadvantages associated with a market economy, it may be argued that social work can and should foster the inclusion of those whom society has marginalised. This book explores the nature of that task.

Christine Hallett   August 1998

CHAPTER 1

Social Exclusion and Social Work: An Introduction

Monica Barry

Background

Discussions about social exclusion and social work are inevitably contentious since both have an impact on the welfare and rights of not only marginalised people but of all members of society, and as such, these discussions are influenced by political, social and economic factors. In this debate, varied concepts have emerged, namely: 'poverty' (seen as deprivation which results from inadequate financial resources); 'social exclusion' (multiple deprivation resulting from a lack of personal, social, political or financial opportunities); 'underclass' (seen as a static and homogeneous group of people whose behaviour or circumstances set them apart from mainstream society); and 'social inclusion' (the attempt to re-integrate, or to increase the participation of, marginalised groups within mainstream society).

The history of poverty and social exclusion has been a chequered one, with concepts constantly being redefined and previous ideas revisited as the pendulum swings between Right and Left ideologies and between individual and collective responsibilities. In the last two decades, the UK has witnessed the importation of the 'underclass' debate from the USA, a decline in the use of the concept of 'poverty', and the adoption of the concept of 'social exclusion' from France, with each concept having taken on different meanings for different people depending on their particular political, moral or academic persuasions. As this book goes to press, the focus on social exclusion is again in the ascendency.

Social exclusion is defined here as multi-dimensional disadvantage which severs individuals and groups from the major social processes and opportunities in society, such as housing, citizenship, employment and adequate living standards, and may be manifested in various forms, at various times and within various sections of the population.

How social work as a profession has coped with the delivery of effective services to those affected by social exclusion has likewise been influenced by these wider conceptual debates, resulting in many changes of focus for its work, on the basis of contemporary political and academic advice as to how to respond to social exclusion.

This chapter examines the origins, definitions and development of these key concepts before drawing together the emerging themes and setting these within the context of the chapters in this volume.

Poverty and social exclusion

The term 'poverty' has been criticised in recent years for being too narrowly focused on income and consumption measures and not enough on social phenomena, such as quality of life, dignity, property and autonomy (de Haan and Maxwell, 1998). Peter Townsend, in his major study of poverty in the UK (1979), also argued for a refocusing of the debate onto relative rather than absolute deprivation and suggested that a modest income, equitably distributed, would allow greater participation of people within society. Social exclusion as a concept, on the other hand, offers a broader perspective in addressing multi-dimensional disadvantage, especially in relation to social policy. It originated in France in the early 1970s in response to the problem of achieving national integration and solidarity (Lenoir, 1974), was used extensively by the European Union in its policy and research work, and has recently been adopted by politicians in the UK following the election of New Labour in 1997. Room (1995: 5) differentiates the more narrowly-focused concept of poverty from that of the more encompassing one of social exclusion:

> The notion of poverty is primarily focused upon distributional issues: the lack of resources at the disposal of an individual or household. In contrast, notions such as social exclusion focus primarily on relational issues, in other words, inadequate social participation, lack of social integration and lack of power.

Many definitions of social exclusion relate to processes which restrict or deny people participation within society, for example: 'the process through which individuals or groups are wholly or partially excluded from full participation in the society in which they live' (European Foundation 1995: 4); 'the inability to participate effectively in economic, social, political and cultural life, and, in some characterisations, alienation and distance from the mainstream society' (Duffy, 1995: 1); or 'failure or inability to participate in social and political activities' (de Haan and Maxwell, 1998: 2).

And yet it seems that 'participation' itself is an equally elusive and ill-defined concept. The World Bank (1994) has defined participation as 'a process through which stakeholders influence and share control over development initiatives, and the decisions and resources which affect them' (p 1). Gaventa (1998: 50) acknowledges the importance of participation, especially when there is a genuine commitment to citizen power, suggesting that it is 'a powerful vehicle for social inclusion, and for mobilising new energy and resources for overcoming poverty'. Participation can either be seen, in the context of social exclusion, as an end in itself, as it increases control and therefore, almost by default, decreases exclusion; or as a means to an end: socially excluded groups are encouraged to participate proactively in efforts to address the problems which they face when marginalised or excluded. Participation processes, however, are often designed *for* rather than *by* those seeking to be involved, thus allowing the powerful to maintain control over the process, and thereby exacerbating existing power imbalances (Barry and Sidaway, forthcoming). Jordan (1996) also warns against the rhetoric of grass roots social action in combating social exclusion which emphasises individual pathology and the 'remoralization [of the poor] through coercion' (p 3).

The underclass debate

Variations on a theme of an underclass have long been in common parlance to illustrate the presence of a residual, scapegoated 'class' within society: the (non-deserving) poor and criminal, dangerous, disturbed, work-shy and idle people. However, as a concept to denote the troubles of the late twentieth century, the term was popularised by Auletta (1982) in the USA. His definition included cultural as well as economic difference, but nevertheless emphasised that such people were unable or unwilling to be assimilated into the American way of life rather than being denied the opportunity (MacDonald, 1997a). Auletta's diagnosis has been broadly accepted as the epitome of an underclass – economically marginal, culturally opposed and personally culpable.

Predominantly under the leadership of Margaret Thatcher, the Conservative Government, for the best part of two decades until 1997, had fuelled a growing debate about the greater pertinence of the 'underclass' concept in defining and addressing the problems of poverty and marginalisation rather than concentrating on more structural influences. During this time, the proponents of an underclass thesis split into two broad camps, those who thought that the members of the underclass were immoral or amoral – as championed by Charles Murray (1990); and those who thought its members were set apart from mainstream society through structural anomalies arising from globalisation and free market economics. Murray's work on the underclass originated in the USA in the early 1980s, but he has advised politicians and policy makers on both sides of the Atlantic since then, including the Clinton and Thatcher administrations (MacDonald, 1997a). His main contention is that poorer neighbourhoods are deteriorating to the extent that a new class is emerging of work-evasive, criminal, violent, welfare-dependent, promiscuous and, predominantly, young people. He bases his beliefs on snapshot statistics which show a rise in illegitimate births, violent crime and unemployment, coupled with a changing and more derogatory attitude of certain people (whom he identifies, for example, as single mothers, unemployed people and offenders) to family values, the work ethic and morality. It has been argued, however, that the concept of an underclass has been politically expedient, diverting attention from the structural problems which exacerbate poverty and social exclusion (Walker, 1990).

In Britain, this increased attention to the underclass debate has infuriated many commentators, who describe its usage and alarmist connotations as mischievous, misconceived, rhetorical and dangerous (Bagguley and Mann, 1992; Baldwin et al., 1997). The main criticisms are, first, that the underclass debate masks diversity amongst and between different disadvantaged groups (for example, homeless people, lone parents, young offenders). Secondly, it does not allow or account for the varying transitions and social processes which young people, in particular, go through in negotiating their futures. Thirdly, it assumes – in the (sub-)cultural definition at least – that its members actively rebel against 'mainstream' opportunities. Fourthly, it does not allow for the interplay between structure and agency, for example between labour market forces and individual biographies. MacDonald, in reviewing the relevant literature on the underclass debate, concludes by suggesting that:

...[the underclass theory] seeks easy scapegoats for complex problems and feeds the bourgeois appetite for panics about the morality of social others and the respectable fears of society's powerful, whilst obfuscating the real problems and causes of poverty (1997b: 181).

The ascendancy of social exclusion

The New Labour government, elected in the UK in 1997, has gone some way towards accepting the criticisms levelled at the underclass thesis and has shown, at least rhetorically, a greater commitment to addressing the structural factors which impinge on the lives of those in poverty. However, there is still a tendency towards ambiguity and ambivalence within the current government about the actual difference between the concepts of underclass and social exclusion. As Peter Mandelson, the Minister Without Portfolio, declared in the summer of 1997, social exclusion is:

> the biggest challenge we face: the growing number of our fellow citizens who lack the means, material and otherwise, to participate in economic, social, cultural and political life in Britain today.... [It] is about more than poverty and unemployment. It is about being cut off from what the rest of us regard as normal life. It is called social exclusion, what others call the 'underclass' (1997a: 1).

With the definition of the problem still at issue, the British Government, nevertheless, has proposed several key developments to further a solution. First, a Social Exclusion Unit was set up in December 1997 (see Mandelson, 1997) with an initial remit of better understanding the causes and consequences of truancy and school exclusion, reducing the number of rough sleepers, developing approaches to community deprivation (bad housing, drugs, crime, unemployment, poor education), better integrating the work of the various agencies involved, and assessing the feasibility of drawing up key indicators of social exclusion to evaluate policy effectiveness (Peatfield, 1998). Secondly, the Government introduced a policy – the New Deal – to combat youth unemployment, which gives employers incentives to offer training and employment to 18–24 year olds, who have the 'choice' of either additional financial incentives on top of state benefits to take up fixed term offers of employment or training, or having their benefits cut. This policy, described as 'reconnecting with the opportunities and responsibilities of work those who have been excluded for too long' (Smith, quoted in Milne, 1998), seems to be a more proactive commitment on the part of this government towards the reintegration within the labour market of the longer-term unemployed. Thirdly, government initiatives to provide employment advice and increased resources for child care, in order to 'encourage' single mothers to return to work, have been at the forefront of recent policy initiatives.

The latter two developments in government policy, however, demonstrate the Government's preoccupatioin with employment (or training towards potential employment) as the single most important factor in reducing exclusion, an approach which, as outlined below, has received much recent criticism.

From social exclusion to social inclusion

Without a clear definition of exactly *what* people are being socially excluded from (bearing in mind that 'society' has no clear boundaries), the term 'social exclusion' becomes problematic and a solution difficult to find. de Haan suggests that 'notions of what exclusion means depend on what *form of* inclusion is deemed to be important in specific societies or by specific groups' (1998: 17). At the beginning of this chapter, social inclusion was defined briefly as 'the attempt to reintegrate, or to increase the participation of, marginalised groups within mainstream society'. Like many definitions of such elusive concepts, this one equally skirts around the issue of exactly what one is being 'included' into, by whom and to what effect. In France, the concept relates to 'insertion policies' to combat unemployment and encourage cohesion and solidarity. In Britain, however, there have been few practical suggestions made as to how inclusion might be instigated, other than through integration within the existing labour market (Silver and Wilkinson, 1995).

Nevertheless, social inclusion, like social exclusion, is becoming a politically attractive concept not least, perhaps, because it diverts attention away from the possible need for radical change and encourages compliance with the status quo. Piccone (1995) has referred to inclusion as 'the liberal snake-oil prescribed for all social ills by those who uncritically assume the existing system to be fundamentally sound' (quoted in Peters, 1997). Peters argues that social inclusion as a solution can normalise and legitimate current structures, practices and attitudes, producing 'normative consensus':

> There is a real danger that uncritical acceptance of the normative ideal of 'inclusion'... as the supreme moral yardstick of social policy can encourage a somewhat totalitarian social strategy, making it impossible to call into question the form of life to which 'inclusion' is sought and devaluing what political theorists would call the right of 'exit' from that form of life (Peters, 1997: 44).

Several criticisms have been made about social inclusion as a solution to the problem of marginalisation. These are that inclusion should be more than employment-related, that it may either mask diversity or label people as different, and that it cannot be actively pursued within a free market economy.

Inclusion through employment

Taking the lead from European social policy analysis, much of the emphasis on social inclusion revolves around the right to work and the desire for paid employment – irrespective of the current socio-economic climate of increasing job insecurity and unemployment or of the particular circumstances of those being targeted. Such an analysis ignores the possibility that inclusion may mean more to people than merely paid employment and that paid employment *per se* may not, in any case, be the most appropriate answer to the problems encountered by many marginalised groups, such as people who cannot work because of, for example, disabilities, or people who have left the labour market, such as retired people (Levitas, 1996; Silver, 1994).

Levitas (1996) argues that just as the term 'underclass' has the effect of obscuring class and economic inequalities amongst those not so labelled, so too 'social exclusion', when solely unemployment-related, not only devalues unpaid work but also obscures inequalities both amongst paid workers and between the property-owning class and the rest of society. She argues that attempts to see inclusion as being achieved only through paid work, irrespective of whether such work is appropriate to one's needs, adequately paid or secure, are misguided and misleading:

> ....even if women, ethnic minorities and disabled people achieve equal opportunities within the labour market, it will still be the case that what 'integration' means is participation in a capitalist economy driven by profit and based upon exploitation. The dichotomous model of exclusion and integration obscures this fact... . therein lies its appeal (1996: 18).

Labelling versus diversity

Silver (1994) fears that a social exclusion discourse, which concentrates on the lower echelons of society, may 'ghettoize' those so labelled, thus detracting from the more general rise in inequality experienced among all social groupings. For example, she argues that it is rare for analysts of social exclusion to examine equally the processes of social exclusion of employed people or of those who choose to leave or to remain outwith the labour market.

Different forms of oppression cannot readily be subsumed under the blanket heading of social exclusion – even though the term tends to describe a wide variety of oppressions, from disability and homophobia to poverty and racism (Peters, 1997). The term may mask the mechanisms involved in each particular process and may dehumanize the different groups and trivialise the forms of exclusion involved.

Inclusion in the free market

Free market economics and a doctrine of *laissez faire* do not sit easily with the notion of social inclusion, the latter inferring a more proactive stance towards the problems of marginalisation. The principal answer that New Right proponents had to the problem of integrating the less well-off was through the so-called 'trickle-down effect', where redistribution of wealth occurred almost by accident. However, this school of thought has now been discredited in a climate where the rich seem to be getting richer and the poor poorer (Hutton, 1995).

Hutton argues for a dramatic change of policy in Britain towards greater state involvement to reduce social exclusion amongst *all* social classes, suggesting that the concept should be applicable to all classes as they are equally vulnerable within changing economic and political climates. With the most deregulated labour market in Europe, Britain is experiencing not only increasing marginalisation of poorer or unemployed segments of the population, but also increasing instability amongst the more affluent. Hutton, amongst others, blames these increases predominantly on New Right policies of *laissez-faire* economics.

He suggests the UK is becoming a '30/30/40 society' comprising: 'the absolutely disadvantaged' (30 per cent); 'the marginalised and the insecure' (30 per cent); and 'the privileged' (40 per cent). Even the privileged are at risk, since their numbers have been decreasing over the last twenty years, and polarisation is such that 'class hardens subtly into caste' (Hutton, 1995: 176).

As can be seen from the broad range of views and definitions of social exclusion outlined above, the 'problem' is diffuse, multi-dimensional and constantly being redefined, and the 'solution' of social inclusion is possibly premature given the lack of clarity about the origins of the problem. Given its traditional concerns with the poor, the vulnerable and the socially excluded, social work would seem to have a key part to play, at best, in delivering a solution and, at least, in avoiding making the problem worse. However, social work has likewise been going through various stages of redefining and reclarifying its role, and, as exemplified below, its current remit may not be compatible with the philosophy of social inclusion.

The changing social work ethic

> Social work fulfils an essentially mediating role between those who are actually or potentially excluded and the mainstream of society (Parton, 1996: 6).

Social workers operate at the interface of, and hence mediate between, advantage and disadvantage, self-determination and dependency, integration and marginalisation. As Parton suggests, social work spans the worlds of the public and the private and those with access to rights and those without. Whether such mediation is done proactively or reactively, however, is a matter of dispute. The Seebohm Report of 1968, which heralded the establishment of social service departments in England and Wales, argued for a social work profession which was proactive rather than reactive and which promoted citizenship, equality and solidarity through ameliorative, integrative and redistributive functions (Parton, 1996). Likewise, the Social Work (Scotland) Act, 1968, which created a uniform and generic social work department within Scotland, gave social workers the duty of promoting social welfare, by advising, guiding and assisting those in need. For example, social work in the 1960s and 1970s was seen as having a professional remit to represent 'socially and economically disadvantaged groups (Shardlow, 1989: x) and to be predominantly welfare-oriented in its role of 'helping individuals, groups or communities enhance or restore their capacity for social functioning' (NASW, 1973: 4–5). There was also an emphasis on proactive engagement with clients to 'develop human potential' (IFSW, 1976, quoted in Mayadas et al., 1997: 2) and to be geared towards 'problem solving and change' (Sanders and Pedersen, 1984: xiv). The balance in the 1960s and 1970s was shifting, according to Parton (1996), from one of reactive, individual casework to one of proactive, collective responsibility for social problems.

Many members of the profession, however, both then and now, would dispute social work's claim to a collective social welfare or social development remit, just as the medical profession might likewise refute its own role in health promotion and sickness prevention (Mayadas et al., 1997). In the UK, social workers are not required by law, as they are in most European countries, to provide a broader service of social and welfare assistance (in relation to employment, social insurance, etc.). Unlike the UK, many European countries have combined the twin services of 'social care' and 'social protection' into one overall local government social work agency (Munday and Ely, 1996). Coupled with the inclusion of youth and community work under the umbrella of 'social work', it could be argued that social work agencies in mainland Europe are better placed to offer a proactive service which addresses not only the personal welfare needs of its citizens, but also the wider structural issues of, for example, unemployment and poverty, which may further exacerbate social exclusion.

However, within the UK, current developments in social work suggest a move away from the collective and welfare-oriented approaches to social problems, placing greater emphasis on the individual (Parton, 1996). With this change of emphasis in defining social work has come a shift from a relatively benign but paternalistic relationship between social worker and client, to one concerned more with management of risk in relation to clients who, as consumers, are seen as ultimately responsible for their own behaviour and their own needs.

Social exclusion as a concept to describe and explain the process of disadvantage amongst vulnerable groups is a useful tool in social work terms, because the concept reflects the diverse needs of these groups, helps to explain their restricted access to resources and offers social work the scope to intervene more effectively in the delivery of services. The concept of social exclusion is, therefore, closely linked to the aims of social work. Social work, in its task of meeting human need and developing human potential and resources, must, therefore, inevitably address problems associated with social exclusion and, at least, ensure that the services provided – or the terms on which they are made available – do not further marginalise the already disadvantaged.

The emerging themes

The themes to emerge from both the existing literature on social exclusion and the chapters contained in this book can be divided into macro and micro issues. The macro issues relate to the overall concept of social exclusion, its theoretical underpinnings and policy implications. The micro issues, on the other hand, tend to relate more to the delivery of social work services within the context of social exclusion, and the problems that social work experiences in working within an ever-changing political, conceptual and policy framework.

Discussions about the causes of social exclusion are ongoing and, no doubt, the jury is still out, but already the proposed solution (social inclusion) is being subjected to intense scrutiny and criticism. A policy of inclusion assumes that there is at best approval for, and at least a tolerance of, the status quo and this theme is picked up by Mary Hartnoll, Bob Holman and David Smith in Chapters 4, 6 and 10 respectively. A focus on inclusion of differing groups within a homogeneous whole also denies people a right to diversity and heterogeneity within society. Bill Fisher (Chapter 7) explores this anomaly in relation to people with disabilities, while Ruth Lister and Fiona Williams, in Chapters 3 and 2 respectively, argue for a recognition that diversity both between and within differing cultural and social groupings is crucial if citizen rights are to be respected. Peter Beresford and Anne Wilson (Chapter 8) also suggest that inclusion on terms laid down by, for example, policy makers may not be the desired solution to many of the problems defined by excluded people themselves.

The Association of Directors of Social Work in Scotland has stated that 'the overriding aim which should guide social work into the new millennium is social inclusion.... The core objective of social work is to help to empower vulnerable or alienated people and to assist in breaking down the barriers to inclusion' (ADSW, 1997: 4). However, there seems to be a dichotomy between the philosophy behind the notion of social inclusion (which could be argued to be welfare-oriented and based on notions of collective responsibility rather than individual blame), and the emerging trend within social work to move away from a more proactive welfare and collective approach to social problems, and towards focusing on reactive management of individual behaviour, irrespective of the wider social and economic context. David Smith (Chapter 10) explores this dichotomy in relation to criminal justice social work, Bill Fisher (Chapter 7) in relation to disability and Mary Hartnoll and Gail Wilson (Chapters 4 and 5 respectively) in relation to social work organisations and traditional social work values.

In terms of the delivery of social work services, from the micro perspective, all of the contributions in this book argue strongly for greater user involvement in issues relating to their needs and care. Only through active and genuine participation of users in decision making processes can those who are socially excluded be ensured that the services they require are pertinent to their needs and delivered effectively. Not only should the needs and wishes of users be taken into account in the planning and delivery of services, but these should have equal weight to the wider economic, social and political context. Within this context, social workers themselves need to be more proactive and influential in informing policy, in ensuring the involvement of service users and in delivering appropriate services.

Chapter summaries

This chapter has explored some of the definitions and developments within the social exclusion debate, drawing on notions of social exclusion as culturally-defined, economically-driven or politically-motivated and on notions of social work as both proactive and reactive. The ensuing chapters broaden this debate in relation to social work, and explore the implications of social exclusion for theory, policy and practice.

In Chapter 2, Fiona Williams examines how far the shift in policy and academic studies from a discourse of policy to social exclusion enables us to see those who are currently excluded as a diversely constituted group made up of people who are not simply passive beneficiaries or dependants but as actors in their own right. On the question of diversity, she argues that 'the issue of integration raises one of the most important political and philosophical issues of our time – how we bring together a commitment to universal values and universal access to rights, with a respect for the particularities of difference' (p.17). In relation to individual action, she proposes a conceptual framework which enables us to 'rethink the relationship between the individual and the structural so that we are able to challenge the all-too-easy recourse to individualist explanation which still dominates political discourses of poverty and social exclusion' (p.25).

Ruth Lister, in Chapter 3, explores the concepts and theoretical implications of the term 'citizenship' as potentially exclusionary, not least as perceived by those who are marginalised, for example because of poverty, social divisions or immigration controls. Citizens' participation in matters which affect them (especially so in the field of social work) should be combined with their rights as individuals. Ruth Lister argues that social workers are well-placed to promote the citizenship of marginalised groups through, for example, encouraging community development, self-help activities and user involvement. She also explores the inherent problem of all;owing for diversity within an inclusive society (a topic also examined in Chapter 2 and 7 in particular).

Mary Hartnoll, in Chapter 4, examines social work practice in the context of social, economic and political change. She notes the shift away from collective responsibility towards harsher social policies and suggests social work practice has increasingly focused on individual problems and gatekeeping access to services. She documents some of social work's achievements in Scotland, for example in relation to children, offending, drug abuse and the involvement of users and carers in social work services. However, given the increase in social problems such as poverty, drug abuse and violent crime, social work could be seen to have failed in its principal duty of promoting social welfare. Mary Hartnoll suggests the way forward is for social work to complement the government's strategies to combat social exclusion by refocusing its work on reducing dependency and empowering clients and redeveloping the advocacy and community development roles within social work.

Chapter 5 looks at the theoretical underpinnings of social work organisations, taken from a postmodern standpoint. Gail Wilson explores how a postmodern view of social work can illustrate the recent tendency to move from the collective to the individual, from welfare-oriented to consumer-oriented approaches to social work and from preventive input to reactive intervention. She argues that, unless there is a genuine commitment to social inclusion, in terms of involvement and influence of users (and their representatives), they will always remain 'toothless advisors'. User knowledge is valuable and only when users are recognised as agents and producers of services will better and more professional services be sustained. However, she warns that 'the full input of users is only possible when their existing contributions in the forms of co-production, service planning and quality assurance are understood and properly managed' (p 60).

Bob Holman, in Chapter 6, takes up the theme of community and, within communities, of self-help and self-determination. He engages with a common theme throughout this book: the growth of the New Right doctrine of *laissez-faire*, and with it a pervasive tolerance of poverty and disadvantage. In support of Fiona Williams' argument in Chapter 2, Bob Holman also explores the role of political expedience in shifting the debate, for example, from 'social exclusion' to a focus on the 'underclass'. He concludes with a plea for the development of neighbourhood groups, which are rooted in the locality, but which require a commitment from Government for longer-term funding and a greater awareness within the social work profession of their value and influence.

In Chapter 7, Bill Fisher focuses on the perspective of disabled people, as users not only of social work services but of other services within the community, for example, transport, housing, leisure facilities and employment services. As with other user groups, there is a tendency within society to consider disabled people as an homegeneous group with similar, if not the same, needs. There is an equally misconceived tendency of able-bodied people to expect disabled people to adapt to living with a disability within a rigid and pre-defined set of social criteria, rather than to have services, legislation, policies and practice tailored to suit disabled people's needs more equitably. Bill Fisher illustrates his arguments in relation to particular pieces of legislation which impact adversely on people with disabilities.

Chapter 8 explores the greater involvement of service users in discussions relating to their social exclusion. Peter Beresford and Anne Wilson argue that their exclusion from debate is both damaging and discriminating. They argue that including the subjects of social exclusion would better inform the debate, would minimise the objectification of people as socially excluded and would encourage a greater respect for people's rights and citizenship. Social work as a profession needs to take a critical look at its own philosophies and practices in relation to social exclusion, in particular in promoting self-determination and empowerment and encouraging a more participatory dialogue about social exclusion.

In relation to ethnicity and 'race', Navnit Dholakia reminds us in Chapter 9 that racial discrimination is still prevalent, even though minority ethnic groups in Britain make an increasingly valuable contribution towards its prosperity. This discrimination persists, not least within the criminal justice system, denies people their rights as citizens and can only exacerbate their social exclusion. Black offenders (and, no doubt, black suspects and victims also) are treated more severely and more unfairly than their white counterparts, for example in being given longer prison sentences or being arrested without justification. He argues for a public commitment towards non-discriminatory practice, in order to regain the confidence of minority groups and to enable their full participation in informing policy and practice.

In Chapter 10, David Smith explores issues of social exclusion in relation to offenders and criminal justice social work. He reiterates the fears of other contributors that social work is losing its traditional welfare role, and in terms of criminal justice, is becoming more punishment-oriented, with an almost exclusive focus on offending behaviour which often ignores the wider influences of, for example, unemployment, low income, poverty and marginalisation and further stigmatises people as, first and foremost, 'offenders'. David Smith supports the innovative approach of restorative justice, which combines traditional social work methods with a move towards social inclusion. Restorative justice is proactive rather than reactive and based on a desire for reintegration rather than retribution within the community; as such, it could be seen as incompatible with the recent managerialism and warmongering which is creeping into contemporary criminal justice social work.

In Chapter 11, Juliet Cheetham and Roger Fuller explore the strengths and weaknesses of the concept of social exclusion in relation to social work and social work research. They illustrate the way in which the concept of social exclusion can not only provide a research framework but also inform a policy agenda. The concept is consistent with traditional social work values, although these may sometimes be obscured by bureaucratising tendencies in social work organisations and the consequent distancing of social workers from the people with whom they work. Whilst social work can exclude individuals and groups by demeaning them and labelling them as different, it can also be inclusive – for example in its community care role, in community-based work, and in preventive and early intervention programmes. Juliet Cheetham and Roger Fuller conclude the book on an optimistic note: that, under the umbrella of 'social inclusion', policy makers, academics and practitioners have better opportunities now than in the past few decades to work together on a common and compatible agenda.

The contributions incorporated in this book draw together various issues of theory, policy and practice in relation to social exclusion and social work. As such, this publication is one of the first to explore the links between social exclusion and social work and to recognise that an understanding of the process of social exclusion is a crucial precursor to undertaking effective and inclusive social work and to informing future policy and practice within the fields of social policy and social work.

CHAPTER 2

Agency and Structure Revisited: Rethinking Poverty and Social Exclusion

Fiona Williams

> We can think about poor people as 'them' or 'us'... Even in the language of social science, as well as in ordinary conversation and political rhetoric, poor people usually remain outsiders, strangers to be pitied or despised, helped or punished, ignored or studied, but rarely full citizens, members of a larger community on the same terms as the rest of us.
>
> (Michael Katz, *The Undeserving Poor,* 1989)

Introduction

This chapter examines the dominant discourses within which political debate and academic research on poverty take place. It looks critically at whether the discursive shift from 'poverty' to 'social exclusion' provides a better basis upon which to research the dynamics of poverty-creation. It argues that, whatever discourse we work with, we need to be able to develop conceptual frameworks which allow us to move away from seeing people as passive beneficiaries of state and professional intervention, or as inhabitants of fixed social categories ('the poor', 'the elderly'). Instead we need to be able to develop ways of researching the complexities of identity and agency but without losing sight of the social relations of power and the broader patterns of inequality through which identity and agency are inscribed.

Discourses of poverty and social exclusion

Three concepts have become central to the study of those who are poor or excluded: 'inequality', 'social exclusion' and 'poverty'. However, each has different conceptual properties. 'Inequality' constitutes a key overarching structural dynamic which can operate at interpersonal, local, national and international levels in a wide variety of social, economic, political and cultural spheres; 'social exclusion' is a consequent process, though not a necessary one, linked to inequality; 'poverty' is a state or condition, but not a necessary one, linked to both inequality and social exclusion. The tradition of the study and measurement of poverty in Britain, from Rowntree (1901) and Booth (1889) to Abel-Smith and Townsend (1965), was rooted in, and central to, debates about policy measures to relieve poverty, in particular, about how to create a threshold of absolute poverty in order to determine eligibility to relief. The concept of poverty emerged from the liberal political economy of the nineteenth century. It moved through the practices of charitable institutions in the early twentieth century and was usurped by Fabians and social reformers who tied the measurement of poverty to arguments about inequality and redistribution. In the process they unhooked it from its individualist roots (in which it was the behavioural or other characteristics of individuals which were responsible for poverty) and applied structural arguments to explain its existence. By the time Peter Townsend's *Poverty in the United Kingdom* emerged in 1979 (the same year that Margaret Thatcher was elected), poverty studies were firmly locked into an oppositional discourse of egalitarianism and redistribution. Through the 1980s and 1990s this discourse was ghettoised and discredited by the New Right, and by the growing legitimacy in political circles, from the late 1980s, of the concept of an 'underclass' (Murray, 1990).

By contrast, the concept of social exclusion had its origins in French Republican discourse. The emphasis here was on the flip side of social exclusion – social solidarity. This was seen as the necessary glue to bind citizens together – politically, socially, culturally and morally. 'The idea of social exclusion allowed the State to assume responsibility for social aid. In the Revolutionary rhetoric, equality meant that the Republic must promise the citizens subsistence or assure them a right to work and participate in public life' (Silver, 1994: 537).

However, it was the social dislocations of the economic crisis of the 1980s which gave the term a new lease of life. The identification of different marginalised social groups falling through the social protection net – disabled people, minority ethnic groups, single parents, older people, the long term unemployed, along with the heightened awareness of 'new' social problems – crime, unemployment, violence against women, children and racialised groups, hard drug addiction, homelessness – represented a threat to the stability of society. The term 'exclusion' captured, at one and the same time, the problems of marginalisation which these groups shared, and the problems for society of social and economic changes which were seen to be fragmenting society and undermining the very institutions – work, family, class, community and national solidarities – which had held it together since industrialisation. In these terms, in so far as *exclusion* is seen as the problem, then *insertion* or *integration* into society is seen as the solution.

Even though, as mentioned earlier, there are conceptual differences between poverty, social exclusion and inequality, nevertheless it is possible to identify three competing discourses of poverty/social exclusion operating here (see also Silver, 1994). The first is derived from liberalism and neo-liberalism and locates poverty in the anti-social and anti-market behaviour of the 'residuum' (nineteenth century) or the 'underclass' (twentieth century). In the twentieth century, this behaviour is seen as exacerbated by a culture of welfare dependency. The aim of policy is to reduce welfare dependency and encourage self-sufficiency – for men this means getting back into paid work and taking a male breadwinner role. For women it means moving off benefits and into a financially supportive marriage. The second discourse is drawn from social democratic or Marxist approaches which emphasise poverty as a lack of social or economic power within an unequal society. Policies therefore should seek to both redistribute wealth and income and improve the social rights which protect people from economic and social risks. This approach has, over the past 20 years, been refined by approaches to inequality which have moved beyond class to take into account the specific social relations of power in relation to gender, race and ethnicity, age, disability and sexuality. It has also been broadened to take account of the international dimensions of poverty – in terms of both global restructuring and geo-political inequalities (Townsend, 1993). The third discourse identifies social exclusion as the by-product of social, cultural and economic changes and looks to means of fostering social solidarity through the integration of the excluded back into the social, economic and normative structure of society. The focus of this integration may be paid work, 'family', 'community' or national life, or cultural, moral or political citizenship.

From poverty to social exclusion

Whilst it is possible to identify these three separate discourses influencing debate and policy, there has nevertheless also been a shift in terminology away from the use of the concept of poverty to the use of social exclusion in research in Britain over the past decade. It is possible to see this in the discussions on social policy in the European Union (Levitas, 1997), in the language used by New Labour and the establishment of a Social Exclusion Unit, and also in the framing of research programmes and in edited collections such as this one. However, it would be wrong to see in this shift a necessary move away from either neo-liberal or social democratic/egalitarian discourses and a simple embracing of the integrationist approach. The situation is more complex than that, at least in Britain.

In terms of the study of poverty, social exclusion has been welcomed by some as offering a broader analytical framework. To begin with, the concept of social exclusion makes it possible to move the focus from poverty as a *relative* condition resolved through distributional mechanisms, to a better understanding of poverty as a *relational* dynamic. In the poverty studies tradition in Britain, much of the emphasis has been on lack of access to material resources, whereas the concept of social exclusion provides a framework to look at the social relations of power and control, the processes of marginalisation and exclusion, and the complex and multi-faceted ways in which these operate. In other words, whereas poverty studies emphasised class and distributional issues, social exclusion allows us to look at issues to do with social and cultural injusticies generated by inequalities of gender, race, ethnicity, sexuality, age and disability, and the ways these may intersect and be compounded by issues of distribution. According to Graham Room, the concept of social exclusion and its use in the European Poverty Programme research projects have facilitated three shifts in focus: the first from a concern with income and expenditure to an appreciation of the multi-dimensional nature of exclusion; the second, from a static account of poverty states to a dynamic analysis of processes; and the third from a focus upon the individual of the household to the general impoverishment of communities (Room 1994, 1995). These shifts have paved the way for greater recognition of the heterogeneity of 'the poor' and acknowledgement of the fact that people experiencing poverty are not a uniform group bound together in time and space. All manner of difference underpin and transect their experiences, including those of time and space (see Ashworth and Walker, 1991 and Walker, 1995 on temporal difference). These developments also create the possibility of creating a set of comparable indicators of social exclusion that move beyond economic rights to civil, political and social rights in order to examine the ways in which people are excluded from, and might be included in, the democratic and legal systems (civic integration), the labour market (economic integration), the welfare system (social integration) and the family and community (interpersonal integration) (Berghman, 1995: 19). In this way, such studies have been able to provide a basis for developing more locality/neighbourhood studies in different countries.

On the other side, the actual political *application* of the concept of social exclusion has not demonstrated its flexibility, especially when it comes to meanings of 'integration'. Within the EU, for example, in the White Papers on *European Social Policy* (EC,1994a) and *Growth, Competitiveness, Employment* (EC,1994b) integration into society means, first and foremost, integration into *paid work* – for both men and women. At the same time these documents also emphasise labour flexibility *and* the necessity to reduce social expenditure – the very processes, which by different reckonings, give rise to social exclusion especially for women, young people, minority ethnic groups, and poorer older people. In Ruth Levitas' analysis she suggests this dovetailing is one in which 'a punk Durkheimianism of the 1990s replaces (or joins) a punk Monetarism of the 1980s' (Levitas, 1996: 13). She also sees resonances of this emphasis upon integration through paid work in the left-centrist report by the *Commission on Social Justice* (CSJ/IPPR, 1994) and Will Hutton's *The State We're In* (1995). The problem with this emphasis, she argues, is that it serves to devalue unpaid work usually carried out by women, and to distract attention away from economic and social inequalities (of 'race', gender, disability, age) that already exist in the labour market.

In a talk to the Fabian Society in August 1997, Peter Mandelson, Minister Without Portfolio in the New Labour government, recommended the setting up of a Social Exclusion Unit which would rescue Britain's 'underclass' from the twin dangers of unemployment and social exclusion (Mandelson, 1997a; Smithers and Milne, 1997). Along with New Labour's welfare-to-work programme (aimed at getting the young unemployed and single parents back to work), Mandelson's speech clearly placed paid work as the main focus for policies of integration. In the discussions and speeches about both these social policy initiatives, paid work has been identified as central to both economic and *moral* integration. In the speeches of the New Labour Prime Minister, Tony Blair, paid work is counterposed to life on the dole, petty crime and drugs; paid work is also defined in terms of that which citizens put into society in order to create the basis for that which they take out. Ruth Levitas argues that the construction of the social exclusion discourse in these terms cuts it loose from any notion of redistribution in which the gains and losses of employment and unemployment are collectivised and shared. It also legitimises the notion that being out of work and on benefits *inevitably* leads to poverty and social exclusion. And it endorses the idea that benefits such as pensions are a *personal* responsibility to be earned through personal investment from paid work, rather than as of right from collective social provision (Levitas, 1997).

In relation to women, although the welfare-to-work programme endorses the right and wish of many mothers to earn an independent wage, nevertheless, by directing single mothers of school-age children into paid work with only minimal child-care provision, it increases a situation where women are increasingly expected to do two jobs – one paid in the labour market, the other unpaid at home. Furthermore, this focus upon the labour market as a solution to integration obscures the very processes within the labour market which render some groups of people at much greater risk of poverty. In terms of the three discourses of poverty/social exclusion outlined earlier, New Labour in its first few months in office managed to combine the integrationist emphasis of the French/EU social exclusion discourse with the 'underclass' notion of neo-liberal poverty discourse, whilst moving away from the focus on inequality and redistribution of the social democratic poverty discourse. It is likely, however, that this relationship with the redistributive discourse will fluctuate in response to pressure being brought to bear on New Labour by coalitions of the poverty lobby, women's organisations, the disablity movement, left Labour MPs and progressive academics.

If the interpretation of integration as economic integration serves to reinforce (in this case by obscuring) the boundaries between paid and unpaid work, then the notion of the cultural integration of excluded groups has also been viewed with suspicion by those who stand on the margins of dominant cultural norms. 'Assimilation' practices for migrants and minority ethnic groups in Britain and Europe in the 1960s and 1970s were criticised for imposing inappropriate cultural expectations upon those whose practices or beliefs were different. Furthermore, where cultures are hierarchically positioned (where some cultures are regarded as inferior) then resistance to assimilation can become the basis for *exclusion* from social rights. Similarly, those who live outside the dominant heterosexual culture may be refused access to rights (for example, pensions, joint tenancies) which are taken for granted by those within that culture. And as the disability movement has argued, integration into able-bodied society means challenging material, cultural and environmental structures to the core.

The lesson from this is that in so far as exclusion also implies 'integration' or 'citizenship' then we have to be prepared to interrogate the boundaries which construct these concepts – boundaries between the public and the private sphere which ignore women's role in unpaid work; boundaries of nationhood – of linguistic, ethnic, racial, territorial exclusions; boundaries of intimacy which obscure hierarchies of power within sexual relationships whilst excluding non-heterosexual or disabled families and households; and generational and environmental boundaries which fix older people, young people or disabled people in constricted spaces. The lessons, too, of the struggles by those groups constrained by these boundaries is that we have to be suspicious of a false universalism – of terms like integration, equality and citizenship which signify inclusion for all, but in practice spell exclusion for some, and where the notion of universalism is constituted by particular, hegemonic norms. In post-war Keynesian welfare states these were, by and large, white, male, able-bodied, heterosexual norms. In other words, the issue of integration raises one of the most important political and philosophical issues of our time – how we bring together a commitment to universal values and universal access to rights, with a respect for the particularities of difference. If we pursue the notion of integration then we have to pursue it through the principle of a differentiated universalism: the pursuit of integration through dialogues of difference (see Williams 1992; Lister, 1997a).

If this tension between universalism and particularism is one of the big issues of our time, then another one must be how people and groups can articulate their claims or have a voice in the organisation and delivery of services to meet their needs. In research terms this translates into the question of how we represent people, and, in the case of poverty and social exclusion, how we give those who are poor and excluded a voice. This takes us back to Katz's quotation at the beginning of this chapter and leads to the question: does this shift from a focus on poverty to social exclusion give any more recognition for those in poverty to be understood as creative agents of their own lives, rather than as objects of policy, or as members of discrete groups cut loose from society?

Sceptically, we might suggest that whilst social exclusion has replaced poverty in political and academic discourses, essentially both remain firmly embedded within a political/administrative/expert/technical discourse. The difference is that poverty was embedded in the liberal anxieties or Fabian social conscience of early and high capitalism, whilst social exclusion has become the signifier of anxieties of late/post-industrial capitalism: it expresses the fear of the consequences of fragmentation and it seeks to reassert the 'social' in a way that ties it firmly into a market-centred society in which needs and aspirations are met, in the main, through that market. More significantly, neither 'poverty' nor 'social exclusion' has become a discourse of resistance. The concept of poverty did not, of itself, create identities of political enactment (unlike 'disability' – disabled people grasped the administrative identity that had been imposed upon them and turned it into a collective political identity). Whether the concept of social exclusion can create such identities with its greater capacity to refer to the multi-faceted and multi-dimensional processes of exclusion, remains to be seen. Nevertheless, linked to this is whether we, as researchers, can imbue our research with an understanding of those experiencing exclusion as welfare subjects possessing identities and capacities for action. And how is this connected to both the discursive practices and material resources of social policies as well as the broader structural dynamics of inequality?

The emergence of the welfare subject[1]

In theoretical terms the problem identified in the previous paragraph is one of how to conceptualise, in research on poverty and social exclusion, the relationship between agency and structure. It may be helpful to start by (over)stating what might be seen to be the characteristics of an earlier paradigm of policy/poverty research in order to mark out the characteristics of a new paradigm (see also Titterton, 1992 and Williams, Popay and Oakley, in press), (even though, eventually, I shall argue that parts of the old paradigm should inform the new). In a simplified typecasting, then, the old paradigm provided analyses of policies in terms of measurable outcomes for social groups, and these social groups were

---

1. The following sections are drawn from Williams, Popay and Oakley (in press) where Chapters 1 and 8 elaborate these ideas in greater detail.

categorised and constructed in objective terms by the Registrar-General, by researchers, or by policy-makers (that is, as socio-economic/occupational groups, or groups in need – single parents, frail elderly, chronically ill, etc.). In general, these categories of people were seen as the inactive beneficiaries (or not, as the case may be) of different policies, whose content might vary according to dominant political ideologies, or, in the political economy version, according to the compromises wrought between labour and capital. In this scenario, the concept of social divisions was generally limited to class, and the concept of social categories to income, occupation and/or an administrative definition of special need. The concepts of agency, identity or personal experience were either non-existent, or they surfaced as the collective class struggle of labour (or later, collectively organised women). In this framework, the outcomes of policies are understood to be measurable in terms of access to benefits and services created to alleviate certain identifiable risks and needs (poverty, unemployment, housing, health and education). Occasionally less measurable terms, such as stigma, emerged to explain some of the mismatch between policy implementation and personal or cultural responses. However, over the last 20 years a number of social and political changes have forced a rethinking of parts of this earlier paradigm.

Shifting the grounds of enquiry

First, the major contextual shift has been the break-up of the post-war welfare settlement – the classic Keynesian Welfare State – committed to full, white, male employment, mass educational opportunities and state-provided, professionally-delivered forms of quasi-universal protection from poverty, unemployment, ill-health and homelessness. Since the mid-1970s, its key organisational characteristics – mass/universal state-provided, bureaucratically-run and professionally-delivered – have been challenged, first by the dynamics of economic recession, then by neo-conservative critiques of the welfare state's efficiency, as well as from progressive critiques of its equity by the new forms of political collectivities on the left – especially from the social movements based on inequalities of gender, 'race', disability and sexuality. However, what emerged in Britain by the 1980s was a new form of welfare regime, tightly controlled by the centralised state, but organisationally dispersed through the creation of the three M's – markets, managers and mixed economies. This shift from a bureaucratic/professional welfare regime to a managerialist welfare regime is not unique to Britain, but has taken place in most Western industrialised welfare states. In spite of the dominance of neo-liberalism in Britain in the 1980s and the first half of the 1990s, different and competing discourses of welfare can be seen. New Right politics of 'consumer sovereignty', 'individual choice' and 'diversity of needs' jostle with the notions of 'user-control' and 'welfare citizenship' and the 'diversity of social rights' from the left, and with notions of 'responsibilities with rights' from New Labour. However, what all have in common is a new emphasis upon the welfare citizen/consumer as, first, agent of their welfare destiny – whether through the market, through exercising social responsibilities, or through local, democratic forms, and second, as articulating their differential welfare needs.

The second shift has been in the forms of political support for welfare. The Keynesian Welfare State sought to address the needs of an organised male working class, on whose solidarity it depended for its political support. Two processes have undermined this interdependence. The first is the development of a more complex relationship between social divisions and welfare, especially in the realisation of the gains of the middle class in certain areas of universal provision – health and education in particular; and in the limitations of state welfare to meet the specific needs of women and minority and ethnic groups. The second process is in the break-up of those older forms of work organisations and the decline of power of class solidarity, mainly expressed through the trade unions, upon which the welfare state depended, along with the rise of new forms of solidarity around gender, 'race', disability and sexuality. The growth of these diversely constituted solidarities has also been accompanied by a reduction in the opportunities for the formation of consensual politics. In intellectual terms, these changes suggest a need for a more complex understanding of the subject and objective elements of people's social positioning, and of the relationship between these and welfare needs. In social terms, the changes also signify changing social conditions and expectations, especially around the patterns of male and female employment and unemployment, changing household structures, and the changing arenas for the articulation of new claims upon welfare. And in political terms, these changes raise a new problem. As articulated by Esping-Andersen (1996: 267) this 'is how to forge coalitions for an alternative, post-industrial model of citizenship and egalitarianism'. In research terms, this suggests an approach to welfare research which is much more sensitive to the complex and dynamic structuring of people's needs, their resources, their networks of support, their opportunities and their social relations.

A third shift is in the relationship of the researcher to policy. In the 1960s in Britain, the heyday of the old welfare regime, social policy research was dominated by Fabian and social democratic researchers, whose relationship to the Labour governments had been close and influential. The marshalling of facts, the documenting of social conditions (sometimes occasioned by scandal) and the presentation of rational argument often led directly to policy changes. Over the 1980s and early 1990s that relationship became more distant and far less direct. To be influential, research findings had to negotiate the discursive balance of power held by different groups – politicians, the media (in particular), organisations representing business interests, professional groups, single-issue campaigns, social movements, international political organisations and so on. The capacity to influence policy depends not so much on the incontrovertibility of one's research findings as on the capacity to engage with and control the movement of the dominant welfare discourses.

The fourth shift has been in the focus of social policy research. Up until the mid-1980s most British social policy research – both empirical and theoretical – contextualised itself within the state, and, in particular, the nation-state. A number of processes changed this. On the one hand, the development of a mixed economy of welfare along with a greater recognition given to the informal provision of welfare (especially by women as carers) means that the informal, voluntary and commercial sectors of welfare have acquired much greater significance (although they were always on the agenda of welfare pluralists from the 1970s). On the other hand, the boundaries of welfare research have moved beyond the nation state. First, it became clear that the international dimensions of economic recession and social changes were having variable and comparable effects upon the welfare states in different industrialised countries. Secondly, the re-drawing of national and political boundaries between Eastern and Western Europe and the creation of the European Union provided new administrative and political contexts for the development of social policies. Thirdly, analyses of economic, social and cultural globalisation pointed to an increasingly interconnected international social order. All of these processes pushed in the direction of a rapid development of theory and research based upon comparative social policy. However, this process in itself seemed to marginalise some of the more complex, finely-pointed research which was attempting to untangle the dynamics of social relations involved in, for example, care relationships or relationships between young mothers and health visitors. This work had begun to focus much more on the experiences and identities of welfare subjects and the psychological and sociological dynamics of processes of care and dependency. Whilst this closely-observed work seemed to provide an opportunity to unravel issues of agency and subjectivity, the theoretical core of the study of social policy had moved to more international and global contexts, but in ways that still privileged the social relations of class and the relationship between the state and the market over and above issues of gender, ethnicity, disability or the family and the informal sector (although this is now being remedied).

The conceptual gap which had emerged by the 1990s was between the largely production-centred analysis of welfare regimes (Esping-Andersen, 1990) or of post-Fordist welfare states (see the essays in Burrows and Loader, 1994)) and the small-scale studies on kinship, care and communities. In analytical terms the problem had become not only how to explore the nature of subjectivity and agency, and the complexity of social divisions, but to find the middle-range concepts which could tie these to the structural contexts of globalisation and the international restructuring of welfare.

Exploring and connecting the welfare subject

These social and political changes, along with the theoretical changes associated with post-modernism and post-structuralism (see Williams, 1992, 1996), have generated a rethinking of the framework for researching issues of welfare and social policy. This rethinking emphasises the capacity of people to be creative, reflexive human agents of their lives, experiencing, acting upon and reconstituting the outcomes of welfare policies. It also points to the complex, multiple, subjective and objective social positionings that welfare subjects inhabit. However, in pursuing this more complex inquiry into the variability of individual agency within a discursively constituted social policy, there is a danger that we lose sight of the 'old' concerns with the broader patterns of inequality and with the structural constraints limiting people's opportunities and choices. In these terms, it is not just a question of pursuing a new paradigm, but pulling together elements of the 'old' and the 'new'. This involves understanding the relationship between, on the one hand, experiential and subjective aspects of identity and, on the other, objective categories which relate to social position and social power. It means incorporating the calculable and measurable aspects of policy and practice into the discursive.

In recent work on developing new frameworks for welfare research a number of guidelines for research have been proposed in order to explore the welfare subject and their relationship to both policy and the social world (Williams and Popay, in press). These include acknowledging that:

- welfare subjects are creative and have agency; they negotiate and develop their own strategies of welfare management, and in doing so help to reconstitute the forms of provision they use;
- the welfare user and the welfare provider both inhabit multiple social categories to which they assign greater or lesser significance over time and place;
- these social categories and positionings reflect both social roles and dominant forms of social relations of power (class, gender, 'race', sexuality, disability and age);
- welfare users and welfare providers also operate within the social relations of power attached to the provision and receipt of welfare provision, and these too change over time and place;
- welfare subjects bring with them personal histories and experiences. The accounting of these helps construct identities. At the same time, these categories of belonging are shaped by welfare discourses and existing social relations of power, but they also may generate alternative or oppositional discourses;
- these processes of articulation of experiences and identification influence welfare subjects' individual and collective agency, including the coping strategies they adopt in relation to both informal and formal welfare provision. This may involve the acceptance of, resistance to, or rejection of particular welfare identities and the discourses that help form them.

These guidelines can be translated and spelled out into a new framework (or paradigm) for welfare research. This framework has four connecting elements:

- the dimensions of the welfare subject which draw upon a wider understanding of human agency and differentiation;
- the social topography of enablement and constraint which the welfare subject inhabits which signifies the distribution and changing perceptions of risks, opportunities and resources;
- the discursive and institutional context of policy formation and implementation and delivery;
- the contextual dynamics of social, economic and political change.

Four dimensions of the welfare subject

Implicit in the first element is a shift away from seeing social-group categories (class, gender, 'race', lone mothers, poor, etc.) as fixed, uniform or discrete. Instead, it is the inter-relatedness of these categories that should be explored along with the temporal and spatial variability in their salience. One way of doing this is by teasing out the differences between the dimensions embedded in the individual who inhabits, as all individuals do, multiple social categories. First, there is 'subjectivity' – people's understanding of their own experiences; and next, their 'identity' – their own sense of belonging. This may involve two seemingly contradictory processes – one in which we impose some sort of coherence upon our own multiple and fragmented self; the other in which we identify ourselves with others and establish some sense of belonging. The third dimension is 'agency' – their capacity to act individually or collectively. The fourth dimension is 'social position' – the objective interpretation of a person's position in relation to wider forms of stratification and social relations of power. It should be noted that all these dimensions are experienced and inscribed through existing social relations of power.

Social topography

The welfare subject is part of the second element: the social topography of welfare risks and needs, and how these are perceived. Mapping this out can help us develop a more complex understanding of the landscapes of risk and opportunity that individuals inhabit in relation to, say, poverty and social exclusion, as well as to possible flexible and diverse policy initiatives that can respond to these risks and needs. Whilst quantitative studies can indicate the *distribution* of risks (for example from the casualisation of labour, forms of discrimination, homelessness, economic and welfare restructuring, including the marketisation of welfare, as well as environmental hazards and crime and violence), in-depth qualitative research can explore people's own perceptions, or *meanings*, of the risks to which they are exposed, as well as the *opportunities* and *resources* available to them to protect themselves. 'Opportunities' means the freedom to communicate needs, exercise rights, choices and autonomy. 'Resources' refers not just to financial, but to personal resources, for example coping strategies, networks, benefits, services. Again, whilst these aspects refer to individual perceptions and actions they are underpinned by existing personal, institutional and social relations of power.

This second aspect of the social topography of risks, resources and opportunities represents one way to be able to create a more dynamic understanding of people's own experiences and actions, and the place of benefits and services within these. This moves away from the assumption that people use, or respond to, benefits and services in uniform ways. It also highlights the particular social contexts which people inhabit and how these structure the risks, resources and opportunities that are available to them, and how they perceive them. For example, if risk and uncertainty are key features of a more reflexive modernity – that is, that we have moved away from the fixities of class, gender, ethnic and sexual identities and the security of steady jobs, steady marriages and of firm moral and national boundaries into new areas of personal and environmental risks – then we need to show how far the risks and uncertainties associated with, say, poverty or health and illness, are differently and variably distributed, and how they have different meanings and consequences for different social groups. At a different level, a clearly conceptualised approach to investigating people's own perceptions of risks, opportunities and resources can yield original empirical data on the question of the relationship between people's biographies, their interpretation of their experiences, their identities, their social conditions and their actions within the discourses of, for example, poverty, inequality and welfare. Although much has been written at a theoretical level about the changing nature of identity, it sometimes only rather unsystematically informs empirical research on welfare.

The discursive and institutional context

The third element denotes a more dynamic approach to the notion of policy-making, policy implementation and policy outcomes, in which greater significance is given to the *discursive context* in which policies are made and implemented. So, for example, an understanding of the recent legislation and implementation of community care policy would, in these terms, examine the diverse meanings attached to the notion of 'community care' and how these have affected the way it operates, impacts upon and is experienced by people. In general, discourses may be political (dominant or oppositional), cultural, expert/professional, moral and so on. Community care occupies discourses of opposition (in the de-institutionalisation movement), political discourses (in cutting back on social expenditure) and professional discourses (claiming the social care model over the medical care model).

In addition, discourses may operate at local, national or international level. These different levels also involve different kinds of institutional arrangements for the formation, implementation and delivery of welfare services which also have influenced the opportunities and resources available to individuals and groups. For example, current analyses of the EU place a great deal of emphasis upon the influences of the highly fragmented and complex nature of EU institutions in the formation of social policy (Leibfried and Pierson, 1995). As with the previous two elements, this discursive and institutional context is both constituted through, and helps to reconfigure, existing social relations of power (for example, the development of nationally specific welfare regimes has been influenced by the particular historical configurations of class, gender and other social relations in those countries, along with the institutional set-up for delivering welfare).

Wider dynamics of social and economic change

Finally, such research needs to be informed by the wider dynamics of social and economic change – for example, the extent to which the intensified globalisation of capitalism and technology has changed the nature and experience of work, the changing boundaries of the nation state in the West, or the extent to which women's claims for autonomy have contributed to the restructuring of household forms. In relation to welfare research, a key contextual issue of change is the restructuring of state welfare provision which is taking place in different, yet parallel, ways in most industrialised Western countries. In some places this process is being shaped by economic regionalisation, such as the development of social and economic policy of the European Union; in others, especially in Eastern Europe, influence is being effected by international financial loan institutions such as the International Monetary Fund and the World Bank.

In yet other countries, the national political discourses of neo-liberalism or new forms of centrism (Britain, US) are shaping the priorities of needs. At the same time, the effects of labour market changes, changing household, demographic and cultural formations, the break-up of older forms of political identities, the challenges from and to newer emancipatory involvements (around gender, sexualities, disabilities, and ethnicities) and new and old creations of ethnic and national identity (and conflict) are all contributing to the constitution, distribution and contestation of old and new risks, whether from material inequalities or from forms of violence and neglect. Old forms of poverty, inequality and social exclusion are being reconstituted in new ways. In these changing conditions we need also to grasp the ways in which these risks are perceived by those whom they affect, what resources they use and need to act and cope. In a context where so much is changing in individuals' lives but where so many old inequalities are intensifying to create new dimensions of social exclusion and poverty, we need to begin to investigate new ways of researching these issues, new ways of breaking down the separations of the individual from the social and new ways of understanding the relationship between human behaviour and social policy. In particular, we need to rethink the relationship between the individual and the structural so that we are able to challenge the all-too-easy recourse to individualist explanation which still dominates political discourses of poverty and social exclusion. Rather than simply reasserting the importance of the structural, we have to be able to confront individualism with an approach which can embrace the indivdual and his or her behaviour and reconnect it to the structural. We have indeed to argue that those experiencing social exclusion have a voice, but we need also to be able to conceptualise that voice in order to apply it to our research. This chapter has attempted to provide some of the conceptual means of doing that.

CHAPTER 3

In from the Margins: Citizenship, Inclusion and Exclusion[1]

Ruth Lister

For those living on the margins, citizenship is often experienced as a force for exclusion, although this has been insufficiently acknowledged in the traditional citizenship literature. Having first elaborated on the meaning of citizenship, this chapter describes this exclusionary force as experienced by those living on the margins – be it the margins constructed by poverty, social divisions, or the power of nation states to exclude from both their borders and from full citizenship 'outsiders' living in or wanting to live in citizenship communities not originally their own. It then explores citizenship's potential as a force for inclusion, both at a more theoretical level and in relation to social work practice.

Citizenship as status and practice

Citizenship is one of those slippery terms that means different things to different people and is the subject of disparate understandings according to the national context. A recurrent theme in the contemporary citizenship literature is that citizenship is 'an essentially contested concept'. It is contested at every level from its meaning to its political application. This is, in part, because of its implications for the kind of society to which we aspire, but it also reflects citizenship's roots in two very different political traditions: the liberal/social rights and the civic republican traditions. The first emphasises the individual and his rights (and until very recently it was *his* rights); and the second the community and the political obligations of individuals to that community. Or, following Adrian Oldfield (1990) one portrays citizenship as a status, the other as a practice.

T.H. Marshall's famous essay on *Citizenship and Social Class* (1950), which provides the starting point for most subsequent discussions of citizenship, defined it primarily as a status. He conceptualised citizenship rights as civil, political and social. More recently, radical political theorists have suggested ways in which this triad needs to be extended to include, for example, reproductive rights and the right to participate in decision making in social, economic, cultural and political life. The latter is echoed in attempts to develop a more active form of citizenship rights than those traditionally associated with the post-war welfare state, through, for example, promoting user involvement in and the democratic accountability of public services.

This idea of participation as a citizenship right represents a bridge to the civic republican tradition which originated in ancient Greece and Rome. Here the citizen is an active participant in governance and politics for the good of the

---

1. A longer version of this chapter has appeared in the European Journal of Social Work, 1(1), 1998. The arguments are developed at greater length in Lister (1997a).

wider community. There has been something of a resurgence in this tradition, especially in the US, in reaction against the individualism of the previously dominant liberal citizenship paradigm. Some feminist commentators have also been attracted by this approach which challenges the idea of citizens as atomised, passive bearers of rights by constructing them as active political agents and as part of a wider collectivity.

However, to be of value from a feminist perspective, both citizenship and the 'political' need to be defined in broader terms than under classical civic republicanism so as to encompass the kind of informal politics in which women often take the lead, and the struggles of oppressed groups generally. Useful here is Ray Pahl's definition of active citizenship (rather different from the paternalist one of British Conservative Ministers in the late 1980s) as 'local people working together to improve their own quality of life and to provide conditions for others to enjoy the fruits of a more affluent society'(1990). This is a form of active citizenship that disadvantaged people, often women, do for themselves, through, for example, community groups, rather than have done for them by the more privileged; one which creates them as subjects rather than objects. Bob Holman (1988a, 1993a, Chapter 6) has been a powerful crusader for recognition of this dimension of citizenship to which I will return.

These two traditions, in which citizenship is constructed in terms of rights or status on the one hand and as participation or practice on the other, tend to be seen as competing or even incompatible. But they do not have to be and a case can be made for a synthesis of the two. This synthesis will then be used to apply notions of citizenship to social work theory and practice. At the axis of the synthesis is the notion of human agency, in which the individual is acting upon, and thereby potentially changing the world, a world that at the same time, structures the choices open to her.[2]

Citizenship as participation can be understood as representing an expression of human agency in the political arena, broadly defined; citizenship as rights enables people to act as agents. Such a conceptualisation of citizenship is particularly important in challenging the construction of marginalised groups as passive victims, while keeping sight of the discriminatory and oppressive political, economic and social institutions that still deny them full citizenship. It draws on a dual understanding of power that social work also draws upon: people can be, at the same time, relatively powerless in relation to wider economic and political power structures, yet also capable of exercising power in what Anthony Giddens calls the 'generative' sense of self-actualisation (1991). The ongoing dialectic between agency and structure is reflected in that between citizenship as a status and a practice. Citizenship is thus conceived as a dynamic concept in which process and outcome stand in a dialectical relationship to each other. Rights are not set in stone; they are always open to re-interpretation and re-negotiation and need to be defended and extended through political and social

---

2. Human agency is defined by Jacqui Alexander and Chandra Mohanty as 'the conscious and ongoing reproduction of the terms of one's existence while taking responsibility for this process' (1997, p xxviii; see also Gould, 1988).

action. Translating this into a social work context, and particularly that of community-based forms of social work, there is a parallel in that the importance of this work lies not only in what it can achieve in terms of practical outcomes for disadvantaged individuals, groups and communities, but also in the process of involving them in working for change and the impact that both the outcomes and the involvement can then have on those individuals' capacity to act as citizens (Lister, in press).

There are, though, dangers with this conceptualisation of citizenship. It risks creating a measuring rod against which many members of marginalised groups, most notably overburdened women but also, for instance, chronically sick or very severely disabled people, might once again fall short because of the demands they face in their private lives and other constraints. It is, however, possible to draw a distinction between two formulations: to *be* a citizen and to *act* as a citizen. To be a citizen, in the sociological sense, means to enjoy the rights necessary for agency and social and political participation. To act as a citizen involves fulfilling the full potential of the status. Those who do not fulfil that potential do not cease to be citizens.[3]

The exclusion of those on the margins from full citizenship

Exclusion and inclusion operate at both a legal and sociological level through 'formal' and 'substantive' modes of citizenship. The former denotes the legal status of membership of a state, as symbolised by possession of a passport; the latter the enjoyment of the rights and obligations associated with membership and sometimes simply legal residence. At both the legal and sociological level, exclusion and inclusion represent a continuum rather than an absolute dichotomy. Thus, members of a society enjoy different degrees of substantive citizenship. Likewise, nation state 'outsiders' stand in a hierarchy from those admitted to full legal citizenship, through those with legal resident status, down to asylum-seekers and then 'irregular' immigrants. However, for those physically prevented from entering a territory, exclusion does operate as an absolute. Citizenship's exclusionary force, therefore, needs to be understood within both a national and international framework.

A national framework

Citizenship is a quintessentially universalist concept. Yet, from the very outset it was predicated on the exclusion of certain groups, most notably women. In classical times, men were able to fulfil their responsibilities as citizens in the public sphere because there were women and slaves to attend to their needs in the private sphere. In both liberal and republican traditions, the citizen is represented by the abstract, disembodied individual. Feminist theorists have exposed the ways in which this image has served to mask the very male citizen lurking behind

---

3. See also Kymlicka and Norman (1994). The position of those whose ability to exercise their citizenship obligations and rights is impaired in some way is discussed by Bulmer and Rees (1996) and Meekosha and Dowse (1997).

it and a white, heterosexual, non-disabled one at that. Citizenship's false universalism has meant that women, black and minority ethnic groups, lesbians and gays, disabled and older people have represented the 'other', unable, in Anna Yeatman's words, 'to attain the impersonal, rational and disembodied practices of the modal citizen' (Yeatman, 1994: 84).

Although now officially accepted into the ranks of formal citizenship, women's claims to substantive citizenship remain insecure. Their admission to citizenship has been on different terms from those enjoyed by men. The template for the ideal citizen is not only sexist but also heterosexist so that lesbians and gays are at best 'marginal citizens'. In white-dominated societies, racial discrimination, harassment and violence are exclusionary processes that continue to undermine the substantive citizenship of people of colour. Likewise, disability serves to exclude from full citizenship. Older people, and especially older women, are also often treated as less than full citizens, despite the 'senior citizen' label that is sometimes applied to them.

At the other end of the life span, youth represents a period of transition to the rights and responsibilities of citizenship; a transition that has been made harder for many young people in the face of a changing labour market (Coles, 1995). Although young people are not formally citizens until they reach the age of majority, the adoption of the UN Convention on the Rights of the Child has signalled an 'explicit recognition that children have civil and political rights, in addition to the more generally accepted rights to protection and provision' (Children's Rights Development Unit, 1994: 3). As the Convention recognises, the ability of children to exercise such rights is a function of their 'evolving capacities'. One group of children who could be said to have demonstrated at least some of the capacities for citizenship through the exercise of some of its responsibilities, often to the detriment of the rights enshrined in the UN Convention, are those providing 'community' care for a parent or relative (Dearden and Becker, 1995).

For many members of these groups, poverty can act as a further barrier to citizenship. Poverty spells exclusion from the full rights of citizenship in the social, political and civil spheres and undermines people's ability to fulfil the public and private obligations of citizenship (Lister, 1990). In the words of the 1997 Human Development Report, it can mean 'the denial of opportunities and choices most basic to human development – to lead a long, healthy, creative life and to enjoy a decent standard of living, freedom, dignity, self-esteem and the respect of others' (UNDP, 1997: 5). In other words, it can be corrosive of the human agency that lies at the heart of citizenship.

An international framework
Poverty is also frequently the lot of non-citizen residents. Traditionally, citizenship theory, following Marshall, has tended to focus on the processes of inclusion and exclusion within the boundaries drawn and regulated by nation states. In what has been called the international 'age of migration' (Castles and Miller, 1993), it is important to incorporate the perspectives of those who have moved, or who are attempting to move, between nation states.

An important element in the 'age of migration' is the growing gulf between countries of immigration and of emigration on the global economic margins, compounded by the impact of 'globalising' economic forces. Anna Yeatman portrays migration to the 'affluent citizenship communities of the first world' as 'claims on global redistribution of citizenship status' (1994: 80). However, it is a distinctly second class citizenship status that is achieved when migrants are exploited economically as a reserve army of labour and are denied full substantive and/or formal citizenship rights. Moreover, the 'affluent citizenship communities' are resisting these claims. Tighter, increasingly racist and discriminatory immigration controls, harsher interpretations of the rights of asylum-seekers and more exclusionary residence qualifications for welfare benefits and services are all part of the battery of measures that have been adopted, often with implications, too, for black and minority ethnic citizens and residents

Strengthening citizenship's inclusionary potential

If the concept of citizenship is to be of value for those living on the margins, the first step is to acknowledge its power as a force for *ex*clusion. The second step is to develop ways of strengthening its *in*clusionary potential. The re-interpretation, in more inclusive fashion, of the liberal and republican citizenship traditions, as the basis for a critical synthesis of the two, laid the theoretical groundwork. Building on that, it is possible to challenge citizenship's exclusionary powers from both an international and national perspective.

An international human rights perspective

The starting point from an international perspective is to develop what a number of theorists have called a multi-layered conceptualisation of citizenship. The context is the changing role of the nation state in the face of pressures from both within (as expressed, for instance, in the idea of a Europe of the regions) and from without, in terms of both supra-national institutions such as the European Union and the wider forces of economic, environmental and communications 'globalisation'. A multi-tiered conceptualisation loosens the ties between citizenship and the nation state so that it operates at a number of levels, extending from the local to the global.

The notion of global citizenship, which reflects at the international level the rights and responsibilities associated with national citizenship, has the potential to challenge, or at least temper, citizenship's exclusionary power. It can do so in two main ways, both of which involve a link between citizenship and human rights. First, the concept of global citizenship encourages a focus on the responsibilities of the more affluent nation states towards those on the global economic margins that lack the resources necessary to translate human rights (as defined by the UN to embrace economic, social and cultural rights) into effective citizenship rights. It is accepted by a number of citizenship theorists that principles of distributive justice, combined with ecological imperatives, demand an internationalist interpretation of citizenship obligations. Social policy analysts, such as Peter Townsend (1995), are likewise arguing that poverty has to be both understood and tackled at the international as well as the national level. The impact of 'globalising' trends has made the case all the more urgent.

Secondly, the relationship between citizenship and human rights opens up the possibility of a more inclusionary stance towards nation state outsiders: migrants, refugees and asylum-seekers. The relationship between citizenship and human rights is a complex one (see Bauböck, 1994). Citizenship rights derive from human rights as the necessary condition for human agency so that the former could be said to represent the specific interpretation and allocation by individual nation states of the more abstract, unconditional and universalisable human rights.

There is, however, a tension between the dictates of human rights and the power of nation states to exercise sovereignty in the control of access to their territories, a power that they are exercising with increasing aggressiveness at the very time when the overall power of the nation state is becoming more constrained. Here, universal human rights and more narrowly circumscribed citizenship (and residence) rights can come into conflict with each other. Conversely, though, by the same token, the discourse of human rights offers a resource for migrants and asylum-seekers that challenges the exclusionary boundaries around citizenship and residence drawn by individual member states. International human rights law, if enforced by more effective institutions of global governance, as called for by a number of bodies, could circumscribe nation states' powers to exclude outsiders through the implementation of an internationally agreed set of principles, including that of non-discrimination (see also Held, 1995). The cause of global governance is also being promoted by the embryonic growth of a global civil society, through which social movements and non-governmental organisations can pursue their goals across national borders. The series of UN summits in the 1990s have provided an important vehicle for the development of this global civil society whose imprint can be discerned in the summits' outcomes. Here citizenship as a practice is also being furthered at the international level in a more inclusionary form.

Meeting the challenge of difference
At a theoretical level, in tackling the exclusions from citizenship identified earlier in a national context, we are faced with what Stuart Hall and David Held (1989) describe as 'an irreconcilable tension' between, on the one hand, the ideals of equality and universality embodied in the very idea of the citizen and, on the other, the 'post-modern' emphasis on difference and diversity. The exposure of the partial nature of the ideal of universality enshrined in traditional conceptualisations of citizenship, together with post-modernism's anti-universalising thrust, might suggest that citizenship is irredeemably tainted by its (false) universalist roots. Nevertheless, the critique of the universalism underpinning the citizenship ideal does not mean that universalism's claims have to be abandoned altogether. To do so would be to sacrifice its 'emancipatory potential' which strikes a resonance for many marginalised groups (Vogel, 1988: 157). Marshall wrote of 'an image of an ideal citizenship against which achievement can be measured and towards which aspirations can be directed' (1950: 29). The question is whether this image of the ideal citizenship can

incorporate particularity and difference as well as the promise of the universal, without which it loses its political power.

Helpful here is Iris Marion Young's distinction between universality as impartiality 'in the sense of the adoption of a general point of view that leaves behind particular affiliations, feelings, commitments and desires' and the 'universality of moral commitment to the equal moral worth and participation and inclusion of all persons' (1990: 105). The first, which is represented by the abstract individual of the classic identikit citizen, she rejects as a fiction. The second is crucial to any genuinely inclusive conceptualisation of citizenship. The challenge, therefore, is to transform Hall and Held's 'irreconcilable' tension into a creative tension between universalism and diversity and difference, as the basis for confronting the divisions and exclusionary inequalities identified earlier. Drawing on contemporary radical political theory, which is seeking to 'particularise' the universal in the search for 'a new kind of articulation between the universal and the particular' (Mouffe, 1993: 13), I have suggested elsewhere the concept of a 'differentiated universalism' as a way of encapsulating this creative tension (Lister, 1997a). It can be applied to citizenship both as a status and a practice.

With regard to citizenship as a status, at first sight citizenship rights do not appear very amenable to the incorporation of difference, given their representation as essentially abstract and universal. Nevertheless, it is possible to distinguish two, complementary approaches to the accommodation of difference in the formulation of citizenship rights.

The first is to recognise that rights can be particularised to take account of the situation of specific groups both in the 'reactive' sense of counteracting past and present disadvantages that may undermine their position as citizens, and in the 'proactive' sense of affirming diversity, particularly with regard to cultural and linguistic rights. Examples of the former are affirmative action programmes and the kind of wide-ranging disability discrimination legislation enacted in the US. Examples of the latter are first, multi-cultural language policies, which give official recognition to the languages of significant minority ethnic groups, as in Australia (Castles, 1994, 1996), and second, the specific political, legal and collective rights enjoyed by indigenous American Indians in parallel with their rights as US citizens (Young, 1989, 1990, 1993). Attempts to re-articulate the relationship between the universal and the particular in this way are, however, politically charged, as can be seen most notably in the US where there has been something of a backlash against such policies.

The second approach, advocated by David Taylor (1989), is to anchor citizenship rights in a notion of need on the basis that need can be seen as dynamic and differentiated, as against the universal and abstract basis of rights. This formulation is useful in opening up the political dynamics of the relationship between needs and rights in citizenship struggles, or what Nancy Fraser (1987) calls 'the politics of needs interpretation' which involves a series of struggles over the legitimation of 'competing needs discourses', the interpretation of needs and their translation into rights. However, Taylor's distinction between needs as differentiated and rights as abstract and universal is arguably something of an oversimplification. As just suggested, rights can be differentiated on a group basis and Doyal and Gough's theory of needs (1991), upon which Taylor draws, is – as he himself notes – rooted in a universalistic understanding of basic human needs which are then subject to different cultural and historical interpretations (Hewitt, 1994). Doyal and Gough (1991: 74) do, nevertheless, accept that oppressed groups will have additional needs so that 'there is a place in any politics of need for a politics of difference'. What this discussion suggests is that both needs and rights need to be understood as tiered, embracing both the universal and the differentiated, and standing in a dynamic relationship to each other through the 'politics of needs interpretation'.

The disabled people's and women's movements provide examples of the politics of needs interpretation that have had significant implications for the citizenship of marginalised groups. The disability rights movement has challenged orthodox needs interpretations, stemming from a medical model of disability. It has also underlined the dangers of disconnecting a needs from a rights discourse; in the UK, disability rights activists have argued that a shift of emphasis from the rights to the needs of disabled people has opened the way for the professional domination of welfare provision and 'a retreat from active to passive citizenship' (Oliver and Barnes, 1991: 8; Oliver 1996).

Feminists have been instrumental in translating a discourse of private needs into one of public rights. This has involved questioning the 'patriarchal separation' (Pateman, 1989: 183) between the 'public' and the domestic 'private' which underpins the very meaning of citizenship as traditionally understood. The public and private define each other and take meaning from each other. It is one of feminism's achievements that it has successfully challenged the positioning of the divide in relation to a number of issues, domestic violence being a prime example, and has to some extent undermined its power. Nevertheless, there is still insufficient recognition of the ways in which public and private interact in a highly gendered way. Thus, for instance, the patterns of entry to citizenship in the public sphere for women and men cannot be understood without taking into account the sexual division of labour within the private. And dominant models of citizenship still devalue caring responsibilities undertaken in the private sphere.

It is around such issues that many women organise in the kind of informal citizenship politics mentioned earlier. The notion of a differentiated universalism can also be applied to citizenship as a practice. Here, it is about creating spaces where different groups can come together in what Anna Yeatman calls a 'politics of difference' which involves 'a commitment to a universalistic orientation to the positive value of difference within a democratic political process' (1993: 231; 1994). Key conditions are a commitment to dialogue and to valuing difference itself. In seeking common ground, differences have to be respected and not simply repressed. Nira Yuval-Davis (1997), drawing on the work of a group of Italian feminists, calls this a process of 'rooting' and 'shifting', in which those involved remain rooted in their own (multiple and shifting) identities and values but at the same time are willing to shift views in dialogue with others. This, she suggests, represents a 'transversal' dialogue or politics.

Translating such theoretical ideas into practical realities is, of course, not easy. As Yuval-Davis herself warns, there are some situations in which conflicting interests are not reconcilable in this way and, by and large, political systems do not provide the time and space for such dialogue. Moreover, there is a tendency to underestimate the difficulties which marginalised groups, especially those in poverty, would have in entering the dialogue in the first place. Nevertheless, it is possible to point to examples of such a transversal politics, including in some of the world's most divided conflict areas.

Cynthia Cockburn (1996b) has written about women's projects in Northern Ireland, Bosnia and Israel, that, in crossing deep-seated divisions, demonstrate what is possible. Her description of the work of Belfast women's centres, 'in an essay called 'different together', provides a good example of transversal politics in action:

> Individually women hold on to their political identities – some long for a united Ireland, others feel deeply threatened by the idea. But they have identified a commonality in being women, being community based and being angry at injustice and inequality, that allows them to affirm and even welcome this and other kinds of difference (1996a: 46).

The 'community' to which Cockburn refers represents the arena in which women are often most able to act as citizens. It has for some time been identified as the site for much feminist activism, operating through informal forms of politics at the interstices of the public and the private. It has also been framed as the locus of resistance to racism. As commonly used, though, the notion of 'community' is at odds with the pluralist approach to citizenship politics that I have been describing. This is exemplified by the attempt by communitarians to revive the idea of a community of common values and collective responsibility as the fount of individual obligation and the glue that holds society together. An appeal to community asserts a public interest beyond individual self-interest in recognition of the fact that people are social creatures who live in a condition of mutual inter dependence. The problem arises in 'determining which or whose community of interest we may be talking about' (Yeatman, 1994: 93).

This question is suppressed by conventional conceptualisations of community that treat it as a natural organic whole with given boundaries in which people enjoy a sense of belonging and a commitment to those with shared interests, positions or goals. At the level of both national and more localised communities, the consequence is that the divisions of power and opportunity, and the conflicts of interest that in fact characterise them, are obscured in the name of the ideal of a set of common values and a common interest that favours the more powerful.

As presently constituted, the ideal of community would therefore appear inimical to the kind of politics of difference with which an inclusive approach to citizenship needs to engage. What is needed is an alternative, pluralist conception of community. Instead of obscuring diversity, division and difference, this conception would place them centre stage, providing an arena in which a transversal politics can be played out (Weeks, 1993, 1996; Hughes, 1996).

Some implications for social work practice and policy

Having explored at a more theoretical level the ways in which citizenship's inclusionary side can be strengthened, the question as to the potential contribution of social work arises. Over 20 years ago, in an address to the British Association of Social Workers, Bill Jordan posed the question that, while social workers are accustomed to treat clients as fellow human beings 'did we also consider them as fellow citizens – as members of the same community as ourselves, respecting similar obligations, contributing to similar social ends. Do we see them as moral equals, as equals before the law? Do we consider their freedoms, their rights in the same light as our own?... or do we make decisions as if their citizenship was different and limited?' (Jordan, 1975).

His question was reformulated, again in a BASW lecture, by Suzy Croft and Peter Beresford. Their argument was that 'the question social work needs to ask itself now is not "is the client a fellow citizen?". Instead, how can I as an empowering agency work to make people's citizenship in society more real? Social work can serve as another building block in the construction of people's citizenship' (Croft and Beresford, 1989). Social work can do so in relation to citizenship as both a practice and a status. Two inter-related examples in the British context, are: first, support for active citizenship and second, partnership with and a voice for those on the margins in combating poverty. In each case, the challenge of difference requires the application of principles of anti-oppressive practice. Discriminatory or oppressive practice is itself a denial of citizenship (Thompson, 1993).

Support for active citizenship

We are seeing an intensification of processes of political exclusion alongside social exclusion, a point that has been underlined by J.K. Galbraith. He has emphasised the importance of marginalised groups using their vote: 'voice and influence cannot be confined to one part of the population' (1996: 141). In the UK as well as the US there is some evidence that those living in poor inner city areas are less likely to be on the electoral register and are less likely to vote. Homelessness has effectively disenfranchised a significant minority. Disability organisations estimate that turnout is low among disabled people, people with learning disabilities and elderly people in residential care. *Community Care* has cited some UK social services departments where information sessions on citizenship and the electoral process are provided for people with learning disabilities (George, 1997). However, overall the article concluded that:

> despite the fact that social services departments' mission or policy statements put 'user empowerment' at or near the top of their list of objectives, it appears that relatively few have any comprehensive policy or guidance which would empower clients to exercise one of the most important rights of all' (George, 1997: 18).

It also drew attention to the role of schools of social work in the US in voter registration work.

The vote represents the bottom line of democratic citizenship participation. However, as argued earlier, an inclusive understanding of political citizenship needs to adopt a broad definition of politics and of active citizenship which can embrace the kinds of informal community politics and self-help activities in which many people, especially women, living on the margins engage. This raises the issue of how social work relates to community and self-help groups.

According to a study by Mai Wann, self-help and mutual aid activities have expanded rapidly in recent years in most Western democracies. She describes self-help's ethos as 'empowering and enabling' (1995: ii). As well as achieving practical help for individuals and counteracting their isolation, self-help can effect wider changes:

> For example, if a group is successful in improving services there are gains for all users, whether or not they are members of the group. Some groups help to shift the balance of power from providers to users of public services; to influence public policy by bringing lay people's views to the attention of policy makers.... (Wann, 1995: 11).

In doing so, self-help can help to challenge and redraw the boundaries between public and private and the political and non-political (Munn-Giddings, 1996). It can thus be seen as strengthening citizenship at both the individual and community level.

A critical issue for self-help groups, Wann suggests, is their relationship with professionals, a relationship which is 'both vital and problematic' (1995: 51). She argues that 'learning from and liaising with self-help groups should become an integral part of professional training programmes. Professionals can contribute by acting as catalysts and supporting the start of new groups, by referring individuals to them, and by sharing knowledge' (1995: 111). Another study by Judy Wilson suggests that the potential of self-help groups is not, in fact, being tapped by social services and health professionals. She contends that if professionals were to recognise and support self-help groups, a real contribution could be made 'to combating isolation and releasing the untapped potential of individuals and groups' (Wilson, 1996: 25).

As Wann notes, self-help is part of a spectrum of activities which also include community action. Lorraine Waterhouse has called for a greater emphasis on community development as part of social work's role in helping to combat poverty. 'The extent to which social work services can be seen to invest in the life of local communities will', she argues, 'be vitally important' (1997: 31). Although community social work has been eclipsed under the pressures of statutory obligations, Bob Holman maintains that it 'never died and recent studies are reaffirming its value' as a tool of preventative social work (1993b: 75). It also represents a tool for the promotion of the active citizenship of marginalised individuals, groups and communities.

Community social work and development work can help to build 'social capital', defined by the American political theorist, Robert D. Putnam, as 'features of social organisations, such as networks, norms and trust that facilitate co-ordination and co-operation for mutual benefit'. 'A vigorous network of grassroots associations' represents, he argues, 'the capillaries of community life' (1993: 35 & 41). These capillaries are important for economic development and effective governance and citizenship. As well as strengthening communities, they can enhance the agency and citizenship capabilities of individual marginalised citizens. According to a recent European report by Paul Henderson, 'knowing how to work with local people is the kernel of community development's contribution to social inclusion and citizenship' (1997: 66).

Combating poverty: partnership and voice

The *way* in which social services professionals work with users is also important for citizenship. The principles of partnership and user involvement are part of the answer to the earlier question posed by Croft and Beresford. They underpin a relationship in which users are perceived and treated as equal citizens. As observed earlier, user involvement represents a more active form of social citizenship in which welfare state users are constructed as active participants rather than simply the passive bearers of rights or recipients of services. The principle of user involvement in social services is now well established in the UK. However, a number of those working in the field suggest that there is still a considerable way to go before the principle is fully embedded in practice (Evans,1997: 1).

An ATD Fourth World project, in which severely disadvantaged families were able to meet with each other and with professionals, has explored the potential of partnership specifically between such families and social workers and other professionals. The underlying philosophy of the project was that the creation of a democracy in which 'all citizens have the means to enjoy their rights, assume their responsibilities, and make their contribution' requires us all to 'be ready to change and to consider the poor as partners with whom we will learn how to respect the human rights of each and every one of us' (1996: 61). ATD claims that 'the project showed us that as people gained self-esteem, self-confidence, and sometimes practical skills as well, they started to see that their views and opinions could be taken seriously' (1996: 58). This enabled them to participate more effectively in partnership relationships with professionals. Communication and trust, with their views taken seriously and their strengths acknowledged, were identified by the families as vital for good partnerships. The experience of the project underlines the importance of enabling 'disadvantaged people to come together, to clarify their ideas, make sense of their experiences, communicate with those around them, and practise speaking in public' (1996: 57).

It is rare that people living in poverty *are* able to speak out in public and rarer still that they are listened to. There have, though, been some important developments in the UK in the involvement of people with experience of poverty in anti-poverty debates and action. The case for this rests, in part, on its contribution to the strengthening of their citizenship. Their traditional exclusion has served to reinforce their diminished citizenship. Their involvement should also make for better informed and more effective anti-poverty action (Beresford et al., 1998). The case has been made at the international level in the 1997 Human Development Report:

> Poor people must be politically empowered to organize themselves for collective action and to influence the circumstances and decisions affecting their lives. For their interests to be advanced, they must be visible on the political map (UNDP, 1997: p10).

The Report also argues that all agents in society, including professional associations, 'need to come together in a partnership to address human poverty in all its dimensions' (1997: 94). Social workers need to think about their role in that partnership and in facilitating poor service users to make their voices heard as citizens. Despite the involvement of a growing number of British local authorities in anti-poverty strategies over the past decade and the significant increase in the number of 'poor clients', poverty appears to have slipped off the social work and social services agenda. Instead, as Saul Becker argues, all too often social services label and manage poor families rather than address their poverty (Becker, 1997). The advocacy, by the social work training council, CCETSW, of welfare rights work as part of the social work task, made explicitly with reference to the citizenship claims of users, never really had an impact on social work training and practice (Curriculum Development Group, 1989). In face of the demands of statutory obligations, insufficient heed has been given to the potential of anti-poverty work as a tool of preventative social work. The voice of social workers and social services departments on behalf of poor service users has been, at best, muted. Restrictive as resource constraints are, social workers need to think, both individually and collectively, about how they can exercise their own agency in an attempt to promote the citizenship of service users experiencing poverty.

Conclusion

Ultimately, of course, the fight against poverty and social exclusion has to be waged at the structural level of the labour market and the tax-benefits system. Nevertheless, social workers have an important role to play in nourishing the citizenship of those in poverty and other marginalised groups. This chapter has argued that they can do so by helping poor users to achieve their full rights as citizens and to make their voices heard and by supporting them to come together in self-help and community groups. The concept of citizenship offers social work a framework which embraces anti-poverty work, partnership, anti-discriminatory or anti-oppressive practice and an inclusionary stance. As a process, it can inform relations between social workers and users; as an outcome it represents a strengthening of rights to which social workers can contribute. If they work together with those living on the margins, social workers can help to strengthen the fabric of citizenship as both a status and a practice.

CHAPTER 4

A Struggle Around an Ideal: Kilbrandon or the Kilkenny Cats?

Mary Hartnoll

Introduction

This chapter is based on my experience as a Director of Social Work in Scotland over the past 20 years. The first part of the chapter title requires no explanation to those with knowledge of social work in Scotland. The Kilbrandon Report (1964) advocated an innovative approach to meeting the needs of children and young people based on concepts of prevention, of engagement with families and empowerment of communities as a positive way of promoting social cohesion. It led directly to the Social Work (Scotland) Act of 1968 which established Social Work Departments with the overarching duty to promote social welfare. It combined within one Department responsibility for working with families and children, with older and disabled people and with offenders within the Criminal Justice System. There is no separate probation service in Scotland. The thinking behind the Act arose from the hopefulness and optimism of the 1960s that social problems could be tackled and need could be met. One quote from the conclusions gives a flavour of the approach:

> We are unable to accept the view that in matters so closely affecting their children, the co-operation of parents can be enlisted by compulsory sanctions. A process of social education on the other hand implies working on the basis of persuasion which seeks to strengthen and support those natural familial instincts which are in whatever degree, present in all parents (Kilbrandon, 1964).

So, in relation to this chapter title, the name of Kilbrandon represents in Scotland a strong sense of purpose, of the responsibility of society, of an integrated service and a constructive approach to social problems. I will come back at the end to the Kilkenny cats.

Service development

Social work services developed steadily over the 25 years following the 1968 Act. At first most were provided by the public and voluntary sectors but the private sector has expanded rapidly over recent years especially in providing for older people. By working to support families, the number of children in care was halved between 1970 and 1990. The quality of residential care for older people improved and the level of services for people with learning disabilities rose steadily. Within disadvantaged communities, community development work helped establish the confidence and ability of local people to speak for themselves. The range of service providers widened and added to the diversity and sense of innovation and development. Local services were established in which local people and service users had a voice.

Until the Community Care Act of 1990, however, social work was mainly concerned with people who were very much on the margins of society. There is stigma attached to social work – both in the eyes of the public and for service users. Since the community care legislation, the number of people requiring help from social work has increased – usually at a time of family crisis – so more people are aware of the consequences of social policies, of social work practice and of the limitation of resources. Although social work departments are often in the spotlight, there is continued demand for their services.

Changes in society

So services have developed. What about society in general? Over the same period, there have been profound changes in society:

- in the economic context with its global forces;
- in the family and the breakdown of traditional structures;
- in new technology and its impact on daily living; and
- in the role of the state.

Many of the changes have brought benefits but they have been accompanied by a visible increase in social problems. Gordon and Pantazis (1997) report that between 1983 and 1990 the number of people objectively described as living in poverty increased by almost 50 per cent. In Glasgow, 42 per cent of children live in families in receipt of income support. More than half the public housing stock is affected by damp, and over the past 15 years there has been a steady reduction in investment in housing for rent. The increase in violent crime, the escalation of drug misuse and the growing divisions within society impact each day on the lives of people across the country. Social work is seen not only as not having reduced problems but at times as being part of the problem. Has social work failed in its primary duty to promote social welfare?

Social work and social exclusion

Social work has its origins in working with people who are marginalised. Issues of social control are never far away. There has been demonisation of children who are non-conforming. It has required constant vigilance to ensure that ideas such as those of the deserving and undeserving poor and deprived or depraved children are not re-created in modern practice. However, it is not social work practice that has caused social exclusion. Economic factors are more influential than any others in determining the proportion of the population who are marginalised. At times of economic depression and high levels of unemployment, the risk of social unrest grows. Attitudes to crime and deviance harden and the search for stability becomes frantic. The changes in world economy mean that for the first time economic growth does not necessarily lead to more jobs – quite the opposite.

Exclusion from the recognised job market is the biggest single factor in social exclusion. In the immediate post-war years, unemployment was not that much of a problem in the peripheral estates around Glasgow. By 1979 great concern was being expressed about the increase in unemployment and the effect on young people. A discussion paper (Glasgow College, 1979) was produced following research into rates of unemployment and the link with areas of poor council housing. It was found that even within a small area of less than two square miles there were some areas where unemployment rates were not much different from most of Scotland – then around 10 per cent. But in the areas of the worst housing the rate was almost double. Even in those areas, the study found no sense of an anti-work culture. The overwhelming majority of men would have preferred to be in work and found the experience of unemployment distressing.

It is surprisingly difficult to get exact figures about unemployment amongst 16 year olds but it seems that in 1982, more than half were in work compared with only 7 per cent now. Of the unemployed aged 18–24, there are 3,500 in Glasgow, 21 per cent of Scotland's total. The Broad Labour Force survey suggests the overall rate of unemployment is 12.5 per cent in Scotland compared with 16 per cent in Glasgow. Within the most disadvantaged communities in Glasgow there are few jobs for young people and many come from families with no-one in full time work. More than a quarter have no qualifications. The decrease in the industrial and manufacturing base and the rise in the 'service' sector means there is more part-time, flexible – that is insecure – and low paid work. There are few jobs for unskilled young men.

Social workers and community workers could do little to help people find work – what they did was to seek to reduce the secondary problem – poverty – and try to maximise people's income from the benefit system. This helped many families cope – within the law – but as the levels of unemployment rose and the cost in benefits increased, there followed a battle of attrition between national government and social work so that benefit entitlements were tightened or withdrawn on the basis that so called 'scroungers' were taking advantage of the system. It was clearly not the case that suddenly working people decide not to work and all the evidence indicates initially that most unemployed people make strenuous efforts to get work although many become demoralised and eventually give up. It is economic forces, not the individual or the welfare state or the social worker, that have changed the job market. However the nature of the problem was obscured by social policies which blamed the unemployed and sought to justify containing public expenditure on the benefit system by suggesting people could get work if they wanted to. Over the past 15 years, the changes in the economy have been accompanied by social policies on unemployment which have increased the division between those in work and those excluded.

There are many other causes of exclusion from the job market and from the general life of the community. People with physical disabilities or chronic ill health, with dementia, with mental health problems or with learning disabilities remain on the margins. Even more marginalised are offenders and drug users. Issues of race and gender and poverty often combine with any of these to compound the disadvantage. Social workers who seek to speak up for them or encourage them to speak for themselves are liable to be branded as troublemakers and marginalised in their turn.

The new government is taking up the challenge of addressing the divided society and rightly so. The first target is education. For the first time for years, issues of social justice are back on the agenda. But a new approach is needed. We have in Glasgow had policies of social regeneration over a number of years. Evaluation suggests that while there was much value added to people's individual experience, there was minimal impact on the local economy or the immediate environment. Many of the people who gained most from local regeneration initiatives moved out of the areas of worst housing, leaving areas of heavier concentration of people with problems.

A study has recently been published under the Glasgow Regeneration Alliance within Greater Glasgow of people's aspirations for housing (Glasgow Regeneration Alliance, 1997). It found that the suburban housing market is attracting families with children to move out of the city; and that the proportion of people outwith the city who work in and commute to Glasgow gives cause for concern both for fiscal reasons and for the long-term future of the city's residential areas.

There has been a lot of investment in housing but the quality of much of the housing stock remains poor. In many areas, there has not been an improvement in people's experience in quality of life as measured by fear of crime and neighbourhood problems. At its most extreme the only safe time of day to go out is in the morning before the drug dealers get up.

Poverty and disadvantage are always relative. The problems in Glasgow and Dundee are acute – and similar patterns exist in pockets across Scotland. Even in wealthier areas, social workers will be primarily concerned with marginalised people. There has been immense progress in many aspects of social work service but I think the sense of direction has faltered in the face of increased social division, uncertain and reducing resources and local authority reorganisation.

One aspect of the new government's approach is that Scottish Enterprise[1] is undertaking specific work in clarifying its role in ensuring that the objective of providing access to employment is pursued. It has identified issues which impede access to work for the least skilled – the inflexibility of the benefit system in coping with casual or part-time work, the problems of accumulated debt which threaten a family's precarious finances as soon as they move into employment, and the influence of the black economy. In addition, there are personal issues of the loss of confidence, the link between unemployment and ill health and the lack of educational skills and transport. Work in the voluntary sector is seen as a route to employment for some. The search to find ways out for young people and the long-term unemployed is of crucial importance if lasting changes are to be made in the balance of disadvantage. Social work should be able to gear its work to those initiatives.

It is against this background that I want to look at the current social work scene in Scotland and the connection between social work, social and economic policy and social exclusion. I will argue that the effectiveness of publicly-funded

---

1. Scottish Enterprise is a public body established by the UK Government in 1991. The organisation's aim is to generate jobs and prosperity for the people of Scotland.

social work services in diminishing social exclusion depends upon the inter-relationship between social and economic policies and the objectives of social work. If economic forces are reducing the number of jobs and social policies are aimed at cushioning the worst of the consequences, social work services are likely to be complementary. In very general terms that was the welfare approach in the 1960s and 1970s. If social policies are harsher and castigate those out of work as scroungers, if they deny the relationship between ill health and poverty and between economic and social change, then the role of social work changes. How has social work survived the Thatcher years and what can it offer under the new Labour government? I will look at these questions with particular reference to work with children and families, criminal justice, drug misuse and community care.

Social work with children and families

The Children (Scotland) Act, 1995 is a collection of measures which offer opportunities for change but also leave unresolved a number of issues. They emanate from the growing confusion over the role of social work with children and families over the last 15 years. There is a deepening chasm between stated social policies and the reality of disadvantage for many children growing up in Scotland today. The latest figures indicate that one in three of all children are brought up in poverty. Even 10 years ago homelessness among young people under 18 was virtually non-existent but since the mid-1980s it has become commonplace. Unemployment particularly among young unskilled men is chronic. What has been the focus of social work over this time? In the public eye, it has been the dominance of child protection work and in particular child abuse, although social work in Scotland has also continued to work with many of the worst casualties of society. There have been improvements in services for young people leaving care. There has been effective work with families in crisis. In total, however, services have been patently insufficient to counter the growing disadvantage experienced by children growing up in Scotland in the 1990s. One indicator is the higher level of mental ill health and suicide amongst young people.

The Children (Scotland) Act, 1995 represented a real attempt to change the emphasis in social work. It was based in part on the United Nations Convention on the Rights of the Child and the requirement as part of Europe to strengthen children's rights. The emphasis on listening to children and taking their views into account is valuable and is already influencing practice. What has it changed in relation to child protection?

Social workers have come to be seen as 'the people who take your weans (children) away'. Public and political concern over child protection has led to an increasing weight of procedures designed to avoid tragedies. These demanded an ever-increasing amount of time – in accumulating evidence, in joint visits, in communicating and discussion. Resources were sucked in from other work just to keep the systems going. The eruption in the 1980s of knowledge about child sexual abuse on a scale which no-one ever conceived of has diminished time spent on other work. Yet we know that only a small proportion of cases of concern are ever reported to us.

KING ALFRED'S COLLEGE
LIBRARY

The new Act is not radical in its approach to child protection. It is essentially confused in its message that it is possible to safeguard children and minimise intervention in the private lives of families, to work in co-operation with families and to listen to children. Social Work Departments in Scotland are using the legislation to change direction. Children are most at risk in their own homes. Research suggests that if intervention concentrates too much on physical or sexual abuse, less obvious but equally damaging neglect may be overlooked. For example, children who are brought up in highly critical families with little warmth or encouragement may suffer greater mental health problems in later life than some of those whose families are more obviously abusive. We have therefore worked to ensure that the emphasis in the guidance accompanying the legislation has been to set child protection within the context of children in need. The role of social work is not to investigate crime – it is to assess the needs and strengths of families and support those within the family network to care for their children if they can. It means empowering families – however inadequate they appear – to provide all they can and to supplement that care by agreement. It means avoiding dependency.

The context of implementation of the Act has illustrated vividly the dissonance between social policy and social work. It was recognised by all that the Act required new resources. There was the usual disagreement over how much – but the facts are that resources for children's services have been cut over the past five years by at least 11 per cent and the effects of local authority re-organisation mean that services have suffered most in disadvantaged areas. The much needed services for children affected by disability and their families are more likely to be available in the wealthier areas than in the poorer areas.

What can social work offer to diminish social exclusion? There cannot be a return to any previous existence. We cannot put the clock back to some mythical golden age of family life. The new government's strategies are to address access to employment, encourage positive contribution to the life of society and avoid creating dependency. The challenge for social work is to test its policies and practices against these criteria and identify how best it can contribute to their successful implementation. The focus must remain the best interests of the child and young person because in the end, that is in society's best interests. The main elements will be to concentrate on what has been demonstrated to work, to assess the main elements of what is needed on a shared basis with those involved and to establish links to mainstream services.

One method is to use the new Children's Services Plan to underline the responsibility of the whole local authority to meet the needs of children under the Act. There are few more marginalised young people than children who have been brought up in care. They will already have suffered rejection and varying levels of abuse. In care they usually move many times. Most fail to achieve their educational potential and have unresolved health problems. It is small wonder that so many drop out in their teens and end up on the streets with little hope for the future. There are many more who have not been in care who are almost as marginalised. Social work alone cannot meet all their needs. Education must ensure it improves basic numeracy and reading skills for all pupils. Somehow all of us have to work together to change the expectation of marginalised young people that there is no hope for them. We have all become pessimistic about what can be done. A recent survey reported in the press suggested most parents feel there were fewer opportunities for young people than there were when they were young. If the new government is to turn around this pessimism, it must demonstrate it means business in creating a place for unskilled, demoralised and often hostile young people. Social work in its turn must refocus on the key social work tasks:

- to empower families by helping them gain access to services;
- to focus short term work on achievable and agreed goals;
- to advocate on behalf of the most vulnerable; and
- to contribute to broader community safeguards.

Social work in criminal justice

What is the role of social work in diminishing social exclusion within the criminal justice system? Crime is of major public concern and therefore high on the political agenda. Contrary to public perceptions the overall level of crime in Scotland is not increasing but there is real concern over the increase in crimes of violence and in drug related offences. There has also been a real increase in convictions for sexual abuse though whether this reflects increased incidence is uncertain. Crime is strongly associated with economic factors and with unemployment, poverty and poor parenting – all factors in social exclusion.

Social work in the criminal justice system in Scotland has not had such a high profile as in England and Wales and there has been consistent and extensive research into identifying the nature of effective social work intervention. It is always necessary to remember that most of the criminal justice system is concerned with those who are caught. Successful criminals get away with their crimes. That is particularly true of organised crime with international networks. It is also true of low level crime where people have so little expectation of resolution that they do not bother to report it. The effect is that most of the efforts of the criminal justice system are concentrated on the least competent offender, the most marginalised, the most visible and the most unpopular. Effective strategies require to be based on prevention, community safety and effective intervention. Prison is the appropriate place for people who are a danger to society or who will not respond or co-operate with alternative sentences. Yet custody diminishes the opportunity for change by taking away the responsibility of offenders for themselves, their families and for society. It is not only the offender who is marginalised but those who are associated with him or her.

Social work with offenders is set within the Criminal Justice System. It has a distinctive contribution to make in its direct work with offenders and its toughest challenge is to work with those who feel they have no positive aims in life. Access to work opportunities is already recognised as one of the best ways forward as demonstrated by the work of the independent organisation Apex[2]. The

---

2. Apex is a national employment and training organisation for offenders, ex-offenders and young people at risk.

role of social work in conjunction with Apex and others is to link young offenders to the new government's schemes by identifying options at the stage of preparing social enquiry reports and providing the essential support and encouragement to maintaining involvement. Social work must also work to ensure new schemes are relevant to the real problems of unskilled and demoralised young people. Vulnerable young people will need more support and longer timescales if they are to succeed.

Social work and drug misuse

Any discussion of social exclusion and marginalisation must address the issue of drug misuse. The user of illegal substances will always run the risk of being caught and convicted but the extent of social exclusion will depend on many other factors – whether they were considered to be dealing, what their current job status is, their age and the views of their peer group. At one end of the spectrum, someone from a stable background in regular employment using a small amount of a drug will not be excluded. But heroin addicts who are out of work and from unstable backgrounds are likely to be part of a growing sub-culture whose pattern of life and culture is far removed from mainstream society.

There are strongly held and divided views about the way forward in combating drug misuse and the review recently announced by the government is welcome. How has social work responded over the past 15 years? I suggest that social work has a good record in joint working and service development in Scotland. There has been effective co-operation between police, social work, health and many of the families directly affected. Services have developed to provide a range of responses to drug users – either as individuals or as parents – and to support the families of users. Most services are community based though some are residential. Given the pessimism engendered by the growth of drug misuse and the public perception that addiction is irreversible, there have been gains. The number of drug related deaths in Glasgow has come down – from 75 in 1995, to 66 in 1996 and to 29 in 1997 (Gruer, 1998, personal communication). This followed several years of rapid rise and was mainly the result of a carefully controlled methadone programme, where the taking of the prescribed dose is supervised by pharmacists and backed by planned social work support.

The total costs to society of the spread of drug use, the scale of production of drugs, the efforts to control supply, the extent of crime linked to drug dealing and use and the costs in terms of deaths and wasted lives are immense. Not all are linked directly to social exclusion. But in terms of lasting damage to society in this generation and the next, the greatest threat is from the marginalisation of increasing numbers of regular users of hard drugs. They are unlikely to be in regular employment. Many of those who have children will be unlikely to give them consistent care at all times, illustrating the inherent tension between the rights of parents and the welfare of children (reflected also in the Children (Scotland) Act).

The debate on the legalisation of drugs will continue but it is not really the central issue. Prescribed drugs are part of everyday life and many of the drugs misused are legal. Nor does it seem possible ever to control the availability of drugs – the best efforts of all concerned only dent temporarily the supply. The key tasks lie in the prevention of their use. Drug misuse has exploded in the context of social exclusion on a world-wide scale, of exploitation and of increased division between those who have and those who have not. The government must pursue vigorously action to reverse the increasing divisions within society. There is a groundswell of opinion that combined action can be taken to reverse the trends.

At local level, preventative strategies should include better education, better health promotion and increased community involvement. Social work may contribute to these but they are not its prime functions. Its main role, in conjunction particularly with the health service, is to identify needs, ensure the provision of effective services aimed at helping individuals become drug free and help reduce the damage especially to young people and their families from continued drug misuse. For some, access to new training and work opportunities will provide the essential way back into society.

Social work and community care

How effective has social work been in reducing social exclusion in community care and what needs to change? Within the broad heading of community care some groupings are far more marginalised than others. Over the past 100 years, there have been huge changes in health, in life expectancy, in the treatment of mental illness and in attitudes to disability. Even so, the disadvantage of people with severe mental illness, with disabilities that impede communication or invoke fear is probably as great as ever it was. The modern welfare state established immediately after the war included three main elements:

1. the social security system – for families, sickness, unemployment and pensions;
2. the national health service; and
3. the personal social services including residential and day care, home care and social work.

Most people were led to expect that the state would provide for those who needed it. Throughout the 1970s and 1980s, long term health care in hospital was free, the private sector was small and most of those needing residential care were in voluntary or local authority homes. By 1985, there was a growing private sector in the residential care of elderly people. In Scotland, there were approximately 10,000 local authority places, 4,500 voluntary places and 1,000 private places. There were about 8,300 long term hospital beds but few nursing home places. By 1994, this balance was changing dramatically. The number of local authority and voluntary places had reduced by 10 per cent. The private residential sector had increased fourfold and the number of nursing home places had rocketed to 21,000. The costs were met in part by uncontrolled Department of Social Security funding and the increase in private home ownership which meant that more people could fund their own care.

The effect of the community care legislation removed the availability of

Department of Social Security funding, replaced access to free continuing care in hospital with means-tested access to nursing homes and gave social work the task of prioritising need. The subsequent cut in government grant to local authorities, the removal of ring fencing for money transferred from central government and local government reorganisation combined to form the current crisis in community care. It is partly a result of the drive to improve standards in all community care services. It is partly because of increased numbers of very old people. It is partly a matter of costs. But the real questions are political.

I am not, of course, suggesting that all older people are marginalised. But many are poor and dependent on public funding. Many are no longer able to fight for their own rights and have no carer able to speak for them. People with learning disabilities find it even more difficult to be heard. History teaches us that the gains achieved in recent years in the quality and quantity of services are soon at risk if the level of demand and costs increase. Market forces alone can lead to granny farming. The best way forward would be a securely based and properly funded social insurance scheme on the lines suggested by the Joseph Rowntree Foundation (Diba, 1996). This would empower the individual and avoid creating dependency. We need a force for social cohesion and integration. We need to involve users and carers. We need to promote community involvement. None of these is achievable by a service which is increasingly constrained within a gatekeeping role which controls access to help. Social work should be an advocate on behalf of those in greatest need, supporting informal care and encouraging maximum independence. There will never be enough money to meet all needs but the country can afford a basic entitlement to a certain level of service. Social Work Departments have supported many user organisations to work to highlight their own needs. They do not want dependency – they want to take their full part in society. For those of working age, the benefit system itself makes it difficult for many disabled people to manage without remaining on benefit. A more flexible system for them would allow them to contribute to society.

In brief, therefore, I would like to see a radical shift in the way community care services are funded, giving more control back to the individual and making them less dependent over long periods. The role of social work would be to assess need and set standards in a mixed economy of care. The increased practice of charging for services to people on benefit indicates a radical shift within the context of cutbacks in expenditure. At the same time action has been taken to protect the capital assets of the more affluent. It will be essential in the debate on the costs of continuing care to ensure the needs of those most at risk from social exclusion are addressed. Social work still has a role in advocacy.

Conclusion

I would conclude that the future of our society and the quality of life for all of us depends on urgent action to reduce social exclusion and maximise social inclusion. The definition of an underclass is when disadvantage is self-perpetuating. The research done by Power and Tunstall (1997) on riots and violent disturbances in 13 areas of Britain found all but one took place in council estates – low income areas with long-standing social problems. All had been part of major government programmes prior to the riots and many of these programmes involved residents. There was some suggestion these programmes were actually provocative, doing little to change the long term prospects of young men.

Human beings can adapt and change. Social work has to sharpen its focus if it is to contribute to the new direction the government proposes. The wider context of economic policy will set the framework.

And finally, what of the Kilkenny cats? The reference dates back to the eighteenth century and a blood thirsty tale about two cats tied together by their tails and fighting each other to death. If a divided society fights within itself, all of us will suffer. It is not just the marginalised who lose out. Better by far the Kilbrandon approach based on persuasion and involvement – the essentials for social inclusion.

CHAPTER 5

Staff and Users in the Postmodern Organisation: Modernity, Postmodernity and User Marginalisation

Gail Wilson

Introduction

The aim of this chapter is to consider the contributions a postmodern approach can offer to understanding changes in the organisation of social work and the impact on service users. The discussion defines users as the recipients of social services – mainly clients and patients, but much of the argument applies also to tenants, offenders or students. These users are vital parts of the system – no users, no service – but they are marginalised by the management and organisation of their services. There are other users of social work services in other agencies, for example hospital consultants who need their beds unblocked, and more indirectly the local and national politicians who need social work to legitimate their concern with social problems. However these groups are not the focus of this chapter.

Modern, premodern and postmodern

The postmodern can be divided into the material and the intellectual. The material describes changes that are taking place in the world such as globalisation, the information technology revolution and the triumph of market capitalism. The intellectual aspect refers to changes in ways of thinking about, or understanding, the world. It is much more controversial since in its extreme forms it undermines the validity of western scientific rationality and so of the dominant ideological view of knowledge.

There is a difference between accepting that the world, or large parts of it, can now be called postmodern, and shifting to a postmodern view of knowledge. However my argument here is that the postmodern stance has much to offer. By the postmodern stance I mean both the material and the intellectual views – a willingness to accept that changes are taking place in the world and that old ways of thinking about the world are not very helpful in making sense of social work organisations today. Postmodern concepts are in any case slipping into modern, or everyday thinking, so that most contributors to this book make use of some postmodern concepts, even though they would not necessarily count themselves as postmodernists.

The concepts involved are more important than the labels used in academic controversy. Modern rationalist discussions of knowledge need to make the distinction between premodern, modern and postmodern ways of thinking, but for most people the divisions are blurred and for postmodernists they are irrelevant. Although the modern, in terms of Western science and rationality, is our dominant mode of thought, especially in public life, the premodern and the postmodern exist beside it in most people's minds. Even in the rational West, premodern beliefs in religion or magic and superstition are much more common than is usually admitted, and they are normal in the rest of the world. In social work services where values of commitment and motivation are often much more important than the rational rewards of the market place, it is unwise to rely on logic alone to understand what is going on.

It is also true that simple beliefs in scientific progress and truth are no longer universally accepted. Science has produced problems that it is apparently unable to solve, like nuclear war or global warming. There is also a growing recognition that knowledge is socially produced and its content depends on who is producing it, not on the discovery of any absolute truth. Another weakness is that today's science is almost entirely the product of Western culture and so cannot easily comprise the whole of human intellectual endeavour. Postmodern thinking takes these doubts still further, saying that not only is there no truth to know, but that all knowledge is a product of given and changing sets of circumstances and that it depends on the viewpoint of the producers. Therefore, knowledge is contingent and contested. At the other extreme the rise of religious fundamentalism is a characteristic of the postmodern world and represents a direct challenge to the rationality of modernism. It can be seen as a return to premodern belief systems or as a manifestation of postmodern nostalgia for lost certainties (Lechner, 1993).

In other words, if we categorise knowledge in terms of its ultimate authority, then for premodern we have the supernatural, for modern there is rationality or scientific truth, and for postmodern, there is no authority at all (Hopenhayn, 1993). Hence the charge, which is not wholly unfounded, that in postmodernity anything goes. Also when there is no ultimate authority for knowledge, all knowledge must be seen as uncertain, open to dispute and liable to change with changing events. Obviously this line of argument has some purchase, but equally obviously there are times when a more rational approach is needed.

Postmodernity and social work

So what does a postmodern stance have to offer social work organisations? First, the identification of globalisation as a world development immediately shows that changes in the UK are not the result of government (of whichever party) alone but are part of world-wide movements away from collective action and towards the marketisation of all aspects of social life. Under this head we can put the globalisation of economic policy which has led to world-wide attempts to cut public expenditure, new ways of managing welfare organisations and at the user level, the emphasis on consumption and choice. In most countries these trends have led to increased inequality (pension and other benefit cuts), raised unemployment and crime and a justification of wider divisions between rich and poor, (for example, globalisation broadens the field for social work but cuts the resources). At the same time the information technology revolution brings with it the capacity for much greater surveillance and control than has ever been possible before. Combined with devolution of responsibility, these trends contribute to a new and disturbing environment for professionals who find themselves devalued and constrained at the same time as they are told that they have the freedom to manage.

Secondly, in terms of thinking about and understanding changes in social work, there has been a shift away from elite knowledge towards mass culture, new attitudes to power, and the emphasis on difference and diversity. Under this head we can identify the ability of users and front line staff to act in ways that influence the outcome of their services. Users as individual consumers (marginalised and disempowered as they are) can be seen as having knowledge and power of their own. If they are taken seriously as producers of services there are implications for managers and professionals.

The material and the intellectual aspects of the postmodern are interlinked but since the intellectual aspects of postmodernity arouse so much hostility in conventional circles, it is sometimes convenient to separate them. The quotations below show that postmodern understanding can operate at many levels depending on viewpoint, but strain and fragmentation are constant themes. First at the practical level of service organisation:

> The closures of beds and the axing of services is not being carried out in any co-ordinated strategic way, but through the chaotic resolution of hundreds of local financial crises. (Paddy Ashdown, 1997)

This devolved management and the decline of the bureaucratic model of welfare and the accountability that went with it means that:

> The public interest – ie the overall functioning of the public service in question – is not the responsibility of a single unitary organisation, but instead emerges from the process of agreement between separate organisations, none of which has responsibility for the public interest as a whole (Harden, 1992: 33).

The problems are not confined to social work organisations and their users but are symptoms of wider social difficulties:

> When each part of society is going about the tasks of autonomy and mastery on its own, in its own way and in pursuance of its own goals, [it] may effectively bar and freeze the free choice of overall social objectives and any attempt to give direction to the global social processes.... The immediate effect of the situation is the emergence of uncounted and uncountable problems of co-ordinating and mutually adjusting the outcomes of fragmented actions (Bauman, 1997).

These quotations all highlight the break up of old structures which were a framework for professional activity and which, however imperfectly, produced bureaucratic coherence and accountability. We may lament the loss of that accountability but it is worth remembering that it was basically an accountability to politicians and not to service users.

Such manifestations of a postmodern world are best understood from within a postmodern intellectual framework. First, as mentioned above, we have the idea that logically perceived 'truths' are not absolutes but discourses produced by different sets of constantly changing power relations and social systems. Discourses which set up users as a form of moral high ground to be called on by different players in the social care market (Clarke and Newman, 1997, see below) are an example. Secondly, there is the understanding that the exercise of power inevitably generates resistance and so results in a certain power for those who resist (Foucault, 1979). Again, drawing on Foucault (1979), knowledge is also power (a concept familiar to professionals). It follows that resistance must generate knowledge of its own which is valuable and exists in opposition to old fashioned elitist ideals of knowledge. A more democratic approach to knowledge is in harmony with new shifts towards consumerism and the recognition of individual agency (below).

A postmodern stance further conflicts with the needs of modern science to define, categorise and generalise. This way of thinking has led to over-generalisation and has substituted false uniformities for diversity. The new emphasis on diversity can be seen as one aspect of the increased importance of consumers, choice and consumption in the global market place. No longer are people expected to be grateful for one model of car in one colour, and equally they are not, in theory at least, expected to take one standardised welfare service. However diversity is not enough when thinking about marginalised users. Postmodern thought has been extended (mainly by feminist and anti-racist theorists) to recognise that diversities reflect structured relations of power. In such cases the term difference is more widely used than diversity (Brah, 1996), for example, diversity between black and white service users becomes difference.

The greater importance given to the individual in terms of choice and consumption is paralleled intellectually by the idea of agency which assumes that the traditionally powerful are not the only important actors in society. So service users and front line staff do not simply receive services, fulfil instructions or conform to mission statements. They resist in their own ways, and they also make policy and co-produce services (Normann, 1991; Wilson, 1994). Lipsky (1980) noted that front line staff caught between the demands of senior management and pressure from service users, produced their own routinised ways of coping which became policies. When users are also seen as co-producers and agents of resistance they too can be recognised as makers of policy. Once again the postmodern stance which can identify these movements positively, rather than simply as failures in the policy implementation process, is more democratic, more realistic and less elitist.

Finally, modern science, including the various schools of scientific or rational management theory, implies that people and organisations behave rationally. It is not difficult to recognise that most of those connected with social work do not act rationally all the time, be they users or staff. Much of this behaviour is put down to stupidity or other negative characteristics by rational management theory – things that better planning, incentives or structures could reduce or eliminate. It is more helpful to think of emotions as every bit as important as rationality (Beres and Wilson, 1997), since, from a postmodern stance, emotions are not the dust that clouds the telescope but are a valid form of knowledge in their own right.

Globalisation and management theory

The most obvious result of globalisation as it affects social work agencies has been the arrival of outmoded concepts of management theory from the private sector. First, there is generic management – the idea that 'a good manager' can manage anything, be it health, housing, social work or a biscuit factory, and that the nature of the service(s) offered and the wants, needs or power of the service users are immaterial. This has been one of the rationales behind the wholesale import of unsuitable management practices (Ranson and Stewart, 1994).

Globalisation has also brought with it the various macho methods for cost containment: downsizing, delayering, outsourcing, re-engineering or, put more simply, diluting skills, increasing the work load and sacking staff. It is very difficult for staff at the receiving end of these processes not to pass their feelings on to each other and directly or indirectly to users. However, there are occasions when these techniques have their place. For example, staff practices may be wasteful of time and effort. There are also services or aspects of services that are not obviously related to user needs. In addition, the flattened hierarchies produced by delayering may make sense in more over-managed services where long hierarchies were developed under different systems of organisation, before the spread of information technology.

However the idea that unhappy, insecure and overstressed staff can deliver a quality service makes no sense in social work organisations where emotions are almost inevitably passed on to users. For the same reasons, delayering cannot work in organisations where there is a constant need to exercise discretion in highly emotional and stressful situations, however useful it may be in the more technical areas of administration such as accounts departments. In social work the front line must be supported *in depth*. This means that there must be a hierarchy which can move some decisions away from the front line and away from middle managers in ways that minimise stress and maximise support for professionals and managers at all levels. Social services departments which restructured under the influence of this fashion (Audit Commission, 1995) were left with no one between assistant director level and team leader. The team leaders were highly empowered but virtually unsupported and unsupervised.

Devolved management and decentralisation, justified as the way to get closer to the real needs of the community, is fine in theory, as long as the service providers have the skills to identify need and the resources to meet it. In practice, however, devolved management can simply be a way of facing users with varying standards and differential cuts (the point Paddy Ashdown was making above). Managers and professionals have more discretion and power – the freedom to manage (and to fail) – within a given budget which in effect may mean they are more tightly controlled. The importance of the budget becomes overwhelming because it is the aspect of performance in a devolved system that can most easily be measured and controlled. Other performance indicators are much more easily subverted. Hence the budget becomes the key factor when services are decentralised, even if the whole process was not introduced in order to cut costs. Budgetary control is essential if the centre is to retain any form of accountability but over-emphasis on cash can have harmful effects on all concerned – staff and users. As Clarke and Newman (1997) say:

> all employees come to find their decisions, actions and possibilities framed by the imperatives of managerial coordination: competitive positioning, budgetary control, performance management and efficiency gains (Clarke and Newman, 1997: 77).

The shifts in the location of power which follow from decentralisation and the freedom to manage also multiply the sites and types of resistance by staff and users. Staff who feel devalued or who oppose change will resist, but this resistance is rarely in the interests of users. In the 1960s and 1970s it was possible for staff who went on strike in protest against restrictions on expenditure to present their action as an attempt to increase resources and meet more needs. The discourse has now changed and staff striking for more resources are likely to be seen as self-interested at best and a threat to national well-being at worst. Staff are now caught between pressures from above to target scarce resources on crisis management and demands from users for preventive services. Resistance takes less obvious forms. Some staff may wholeheartedly accept the new resource-driven discourse and pass costs on to users (and those many potential users who are declared ineligible for highly targeted services). Others bend guidelines in their own ways, often in favour of good professional practice as they see it. As a result, decentralisation means discretion to resist, as well as to manage, with consequent variations in type and quality of services.

In other words, diversity in service standards is now built into the system. When there is no safety in hierarchy, no security in the old fashioned ways of keeping to the rules, covering your back and abiding by the red tape, there is no reason to standardise behaviour. In any case the rules are no longer as clear as they were (except for financial imperatives) and so a whole range of diverse responses to change and to service provision begin to be institutionalised.

Apart from the organisational fashions associated with private sector management theory, there is also the passionate and frequently irrational belief in the virtues of competition, which passes as economic rationality. Private sector management theory assumes that benefits result from competition, as indeed they sometimes do. However, even private sector theorists have recognised that trust is a much better mechanism for coordinating production in terms of efficiency and effectiveness (Sako, 1992) than competition. In 1990, after decades of exhorting social services (health, social work and housing above all) to co-operate with each other, the power of economic ideology was so strong that a competitive market was assumed in the NHS and Community Care Act. The fact that co-operation is essential for high quality services and has always been difficult to maintain across agencies, made the 1990 reforms so clearly misguided that even Conservative ministers had come to have second thoughts on 'the market' by 1993 when it was to be fully implemented:

References to the 'purchaser/provider split' ...convey an image of 'stand off' relationships. That is not what we want...Market relationships in the private sector.... are built on partnership and long term agreements. I believe we can learn a lot from private sector experiences in the area. (Mahwinney, 1993, quoted in Wistow et al., 1996: 170)

Another weakness of competition in an environment where budgets are capped and there are no profits to be made (only the threat of closure through loss of contracts), is that innovation becomes very difficult. Organisations cannot afford to take risks unless they can be sure they will get another contract, so they are unlikely to develop new services, however great the need (Clarke and Newman, 1997). Competition also encourages secrecy. As Foucault noted (Sheridan, 1980) secrecy is power, and when information needed by service users, such as eligibility criteria and outcome measures, become commercial secrets, users are further disempowered.

Users in discourse

In terms of discourse, users have emerged from virtual invisibility to new and highly contradictory positions. As Clarke and Newman (1997) say, they have been converted into a kind of moral high ground. Managers, professionals, service providers and service purchasers are all liable to use the needs and wishes of their users to justify or legitimise their actions and plans. Users who give advice in consultation exercises or sit on advisory groups have been co-opted into the structure of social work provision. They are often not expected to cause too much trouble. Alternatively they may have a symbolic role as service bashers who can be relied on to make a lot of noise and diffuse anger, but to have little effect. In some ways the new discourses are worse than old fashioned co-option because the users may not even need to be present, only to be represented by tables of satisfaction or surveys indicating demand for a different type of service.

However, several questions emerge. Who or what are the 'users'? How diverse are they and what role does difference play in that diversity? The possibility of conflict of interests between users and their carers is well known but still often ignored. Other sources of conflict have received even less attention. Service provision can create division within and between groups of users, for example between younger and older disabled people or between Turkish migrants and Kurdish refugees. The same service for all is not equal to an equal service for all (Ahmad and Atkin, 1996) and structured differences in need cannot be met by individual assessment. The ethnic minority literature on community care is more advanced than the mainstream in this area. The analysis of ethnicity in relation to care services ideally should include analyses of diversity and difference in the dominant and other white groups as well as a clearer understanding of black and Asian groups.

Users are not only diverse but there is a danger that user participation in service planning will replicate differences of status or gender so that marginalised groups among minorities become still further marginalised by a system that recognises the powerful within their ethnic groups but ignores the less powerful. The needs of users may also be misrepresented by professionals and managers who do not understand the culture of the people they are assessing – again this is not just a problem for black users. It may also arise across classes, regions or gender. As Ahmad and Atkin (1996) state, staff need to be aware and critical of their own biases and prejudices.

Structural barriers to participation vary depending on the service and the type of participation desired, but they exist for all marginalised service users. At present, lack of information appears to be seen as the major structural barrier facing minorities and the addition of information in minority languages is often assumed (very optimistically) to be a solution.

Practical and positive aspects of a postmodern approach to social work

It is easy to produce a negative analysis of postmodern social work organisations but much more difficult to be positive or to see how to improve things. I would argue that the positive side is essential if we are to take a democratic approach to the production of knowledge. We have only to think of the fury of tenants when their estate is described as a slum, or the unwillingness of so many service users to label themselves as old or mentally ill, or the hostility of staff to being told that they are the instruments of state oppression of the disadvantaged. Such one-sided analyses, positive or negative, can be essential to make a particular point but they usually represent the view from above, and the power relations that produced them need to be clarified. Modernist approaches attempt to be 'objective' and so are usually top down in the ways that they define a problem and produce a solution. In contrast, postmodern analyses accept that power relations are ever present and that their influence on the generation of knowledge must be identified and clearly spelt out.

So what is on offer on the positive side? A first step is to recognise the inputs of users and to manage them consciously instead of by default. This is anathema to those who regard all management as manipulative exploitation, but the organisational alternatives are a return to bureaucratic hierarchy, or management drift, since non-hierarchical co-operatives are not a realistic option for most large social work agencies.

Service users and, where relevant, their carers are *co-producers of the service* (Normann, 1991; Wilson, 1994). They do a great deal of the physical work involved, either as self carers or as carers. What they do and how difficult or demanding it is varies with the social service under consideration, the state of the budget and their own capacities or expectations. Whether it is minor repairs in housing, taking medication in mental health or avoiding re-offending in probation, to take just a few examples, without user input most services could not function.

An example of the way managers are changing the role of users in service production is the 'inpatient episode', as a hospital visit is now known. Whereas in the past patients were usually expected to be entirely passive and to take virtually no responsibility for their stay in hospital, they are now important actors. In the past, patients were admitted the day before an operation so that they could be checked and the hospital could be sure that they did not eat anything before an anaesthetic, since if they did they might die. Hospital clothing was provided. Now the patient is told to arrive on the day of the operation without having eaten and bringing their own clothes – and cash for a deposit on any equipment which is likely to be needed when they are discharged. After treatment they will dress in their own clothes and arrange for someone to collect them who can stay with them until danger from reaction to the anaesthetic has worn off and look after them during their period of convalescence. All this was formerly done by the hospital staff. The boundary between the part of the service produced by the patient and the part produced by the health service has moved dramatically. This shift has only been possible because standards of living have risen, patients have come to be seen as slightly less lowly, cost cutting has demanded shorter hospital stays and a range of new structures for informing and monitoring patients has been put in place.

The above example shows how changes in patient management have shifted costs to patients but at the same time patients now have more autonomy in how they arrive at and leave hospital and how they convalesce. The worry is that patients have changed from being seen as wholly passive and irresponsible to highly responsible but still compliant. Surveillance has decreased but conformity is still required. For success, such a change depends on the ability of managers to take diversity into account and to develop procedures to deal with patients who for some reason or other cannot fit the standard model of behaviour. Ideally more choice and less compulsion should be offered but that would involve more resources which might be better used elsewhere.

The self-care provided by users and carers usually includes aspects of *care management and care packaging*. This work can be built on or ignored by professionals. In social services, for example, assessment makes much greater demands on users than the old system of determining eligibility for a service. It is now up to users to give the correct (professionally relevant) information to assessors or care planners/managers, if they are to receive appropriate services. Professionals usually have very little time to gain trust and develop understanding so the input from users can be crucial. Older people, to take one client group, often fail to understand how their needs should be presented. Arguably this does not much matter, since in most cases their service will be determined by financial constraints and not by their needs, but in theory a better understanding of needs should result in a better distribution of scarce resources and so in greater efficiency. It follows that managers must either give assessors and care planners more time per service user or some other way has to be found that will help users to present their needs more clearly to professionals if service quality is to improve.

Ideas of agency and power are helpful in recognising the inputs of users. The recognition of users' work in service production makes it easier to understand the resistance of many users to taking part in service planning and quality assurance. Many see no reason why they should undertake more unpaid work than they already do for the services they receive. They tend to voice the view that the professionals should get on with the jobs they are paid to do – in other words users are old fashioned modernists (Lankshear and Giarchi, 1995; Thornton and Tozer, 1995).

Most services now have to *consult with their users* in some way or other. If users knew the reluctance of so many service providers actually to engage in dialogue with them (as opposed to members of voluntary organisations purporting to represent users) they might feel more powerful. As it is there are many genuine constraints on effective consultation even without considering the reluctance of many users and some professionals. Consultation is time-consuming and expensive and one way of reducing user input, especially from the most marginalised, is to fail to pay for attendance at planning or consultation meetings. Users may be given travel expenses and even provided with replacements if they are carers, but consultation is still under-funded. However the chances are high that if users were asked whether more money should be spent on services or consultation, the majority would go for services.

In terms of *quality assurance*, the main task of users is to respond to various forms of enquiry about their service satisfaction (Carr-Hill, 1995). Purchasers are expected to monitor the services they buy and to see that they are delivered according to specification. Providers need quality reports as part of their next bid for service contracts. The more forward-thinking purchasers may be able to build service monitoring into a contract as a task to be performed by the providers (and users), thereby entirely shifting the cost onto the users and providers. The exercise may still have some symbolic use – if staff know the users are going to be asked about their service they will hopefully try a bit harder. But staff who deliberately provide a poor service or abuse users will almost certainly take steps to prevent reporting. As Carr-Hill (1995) states, the vast majority of users do not take the opportunity to criticise their services and it is hard to see user input to quality assurance as empowering in any way.

The most demanding and stressful contribution of users to service quality is to *register complaints*. This again is a very important symbolic activity and the statutory right to complain is arguably the one real shift in power between service providers and users that recent legislation has produced. Even with systems of mandatory complaints procedures, ombudsmen and various other statutory arrangements in favour of 'consumers' (Dean, 1996), the stress involved in making a complaint is very great, especially for those who are frail, unused to dealing with the system, or otherwise marginalised.

Attempts to encourage an organisational culture where an increase in complaints is seen as a sign of a better service, are good in theory but are difficult for managers to produce in practice. Theoretically such a service is one in which users are taking a greater part and staff are producing a more open culture of partnership, but in practice it is only to be expected that staff will want to defuse complaints rather than take them forward. Managers who can set up and use an informal complaints system seem more likely to get good results.

More power for marginalised users

At present users are managed from above. As co-workers in the service they are on much the same level as front line workers but their position is worse because they are not members of the organisation and they do not have opportunities for training or trade union representation. Their complaints are not likely to be welcome. One well known textbook suggests classifying users who complain according to the damage they can do into the unstoppable, the buy-offable, and the neglectable (Harrow and Shaw, 1992). They note that membership of these groups will change – especially in terms of scandals and political shifts. The classification is not a recipe for quality user management but I suspect it is close to reality in most organisations and it does at least recognise the power of some users.

It is clear that as long as users and carers are confined to the role of front line workers or toothless advisors, their ability to act is strictly limited. Users need to be in positions of formal power. This is possible when they become board members in voluntary sector agencies but only if they are present in large enough numbers to have an impact and are not merely token representatives. In services where there is no board, the equivalent may have to be set up. Since involving users is often time-consuming and hence expensive it could only be done by making sure that all services comply, otherwise those that do not will have an advantage in cost terms. Purchasers could insist that no contracts for any social service are given unless the contracting agency had at least 50 per cent users on its board of management. This would almost certainly cause a lot of problems to existing organisations and ways of working and is only likely if it is introduced by legislation.

Conclusions

A postmodern stance therefore lets us see that we are not alone in facing management and resource problems which have a negative impact on marginalised users, but that these are part of a world-wide trend. The ability to see service users as agents and producers of services and knowledge is an important part of building better and more professional services in the future.

Whatever happens in the future, however, knowledge is power and professionals who have knowledge will still be the most powerful influences on service outcome and quality for individual users. It follows that no amount of organisational change can improve services for users without the good will and dedication of front line workers and even more important, since front line workers cannot carry the whole morality of their service, without the back up of managers at all levels in the organisation. Managers, in turn, will need the support of the politicians and governing body members who are ultimately responsible. The postmodern social work organisation therefore presents the opportunity for a new professionalism which is able to admit that user knowledge is valuable and that users can assist in service development. However the full input of users is only possible when their existing contributions in the forms of co-production, service planning and quality assurance are understood and properly managed.

Users in the postmodern social service have a legitimacy which they have not had before, but when users are frail, mentally ill or otherwise stigmatised and see themselves as such, something more is needed. Consumer power is meant to substitute for hierarchy, and competition is meant to ensure that services are developed with users in mind, but they are not necessarily successful. The postmodern organisation offers the chance for users to take part in the organisation: fluidity and lack of hierarchy open up opportunities – to sit on committees, to be consulted, and to complain and be listened to and get redress. The trouble is that, as mechanisms, these can be even worse than hierarchy at delivering quality for people who are frail, poor or socially stigmatised. Such systems allow elitist managers and professionals to point to structures of user involvement, but the structures can be very easily subverted.

Finally, the concept of users must include diversity and difference. Minority writers have highlighted a problem that is often assumed away within the dominant majority. Communities and groups have their own power hierarchies, and representation by the powerful will suppress others – often women or older people, or relegate them to tea making and similar low status support activities. Representation by marginalised members of a group may fail to carry credibility, either with service users or their own community, and worse still may lay them open to victimisation. So are trained user representatives essential? The answer today is probably yes. When the number of user representatives is strictly limited, a loud and politically aware voice is essential. The downside is that a focus on disadvantage produces a victim-oriented discourse and denies users the self respect that comes from not being victims. Being a user can only be seen as normal when there are large numbers of users who can support one another in positions of organisational power – for example, as members of a management board. They are unlikely to speak with one voice but their presence is essential if social work is to progress.

CHAPTER 6
Neighbourhoods and Exclusion
Bob Holman

During the last world war, over five million people were evacuated in Britain. The children mostly went from urban, often poor areas to county towns and country villages. In Cambridge, it was found that most evacuees were better fed, more comfortable, even happy in their foster homes. Yet most wanted to go home. It was not just that they missed their parents but also that they missed their neighbourhoods, the familiar streets and the fish and chip shops (Issacs, 1941). I know because I was an evacuee who returned eight times. I preferred our familiar, bombed, London neighbourhood to the safety of the countryside.

The advantages of neighbourhood
Jeremy Seabrook defines neighbourhood as 'an area where the majority of people know by sight most of those who live there and probably recognise everyone of their own age group [and] know all the significant buildings' (cited by Henderson, 1995: 14). Like Seabrook, I prefer the term 'neighbourhood' to 'community' which now has a much larger connotation because of its association with the European Economic Community. The essence of neighbourhood is that geographically it is small, while relationships are numerous. Neighbourhood should not be over-romanticised. There was no golden age when crime was non-existent and neighbours never quarrelled. East London is often held up as a place where neighbourhood links were strong yet accounts by General Booth in the nineteenth century and by George Lansbury in the early part of this century show it was also a place where life could be ugly, cruel and short (Booth, 1889; Lansbury, 1928). None-the-less, working class neighbourhoods could be a source of strength precisely because residents could not easily move away. The results were as follows:

- relatives tended to be on hand. In my London family, the males tended to share the same occupation – as removal men. We visited or were visited by relatives on at least four days a week. When our home was twice bombed it was taken for granted that we all moved in with Nan;
- neighbours were well known. Neighbours came in every Saturday night to our home to play cards. Of course, arguments occurred between some neighbours while friendships were made with others. Apart from relatives, leisure was spent mainly with neighbours. Consequently, when need arose they were sources of help;
- neighbourhoods sometimes provided an avenue to jobs. In East London, many men worked in the docks and they informed friends when vacancies arose.

Following the last war with many families moved from inner cities to outlying estates and with greater private home ownership, an academic debate revolved

62

around the question of whether neighbourhood – or community – was in decline. Numerous studies were published with the most famous being those by Wilmott and Young (l957). Generally it was concluded that greater mobility meant that individuals did spend less time in their own neighbourhoods and did shift neighbourhoods more often. But it was also found that greater car and phone ownership enabled relatives and friends to maintain contact.

Interestingly, just when the vitality of neighbourhood was being questioned by sociologists so social workers began to perceive its usefulness in regard to their clients. Following the Ingleby Report of 1960, some Children's Departments experimented with Family Advice Centres as a means of strengthening families whose children might come into care (1960). A study found that their location in the midst of deprived neighbourhoods did make them more accessible to and acceptable to the families (Leissner et al., 1971). Meanwhile the Seebohm Report had been published with whole chapters devoted to prevention and the community (1968). Following the re-organisation of the personal social services, and during the heady days of the 1970s, some Social Services Departments and Social Work Departments decentralised staff into neighbourhood teams and established neighbourhood family centres. This community social work, as it became called, was sanctioned and encouraged by the Barclay Report which defined, community social work as that which 'seeks to tap into, support, enable and underpin the local networks of formal and informal relationships which constitute our basic definition of community' (NISW, 1982, para 23). As I have explained elsewhere, some social work teams not only located themselves in deprived neighbourhoods but co-operated successfully with local voluntary groups (Holman, l993a). But the summer of community social work was brief. It was replaced by a winter of budgetary restraint, a child care shaped by child abuse, and a social work dominated by central management.

The decline of neighbourhood

Simultaneously, just as statutory social work was withdrawing its focus on neighbourhood so wider economic and social policies were making life harder for the residents of deprived areas. Partly this was due to global economic forces and national policies which crossed party political boundaries and resulted in the closure of labour intensive industries, such as the docks, coal mines and steel works, which had provided both employment and pride for certain highly populated urban complexes. But there was more to it than that. From 1979, Britain fell into the political grip of what was called the New Right. Drawing upon Hayek (1944) and Friedman (1962), it was built around the following tenets:

• state action was inefficient and demoralising and should be dismantled as completely as possible;
• virtually all means of production and distribution of goods, services (including welfare services) and rewards should be left to the untrammelled free market, that is to private enterprise. The laws of demand and supply not morality should reign with some New Right members pursuing their

arguments to the logical conclusion that hard drugs, along with everything else, should be left to the market;
* the main objective of government should be to free individuals. Individual motivation, even though dominated by selfishness, was the best means of achieving wealth for the nation.

It must be acknowledged that the New Right doctrines did have positive aspects. Organisations sharpened their targets, waste was reduced and managerial skills were emphasised. New Right activists did condemn the repression of individual liberty in soviet countries. But they also did enormous damage. First, they escalated unemployment. Market forces and the drive for high returns for directors and shareholders pushed companies into paying low wages for front-line staff and the shedding of much labour. These policies particularly hit deprived neighbourhoods in which lived many manual workers.

Secondly, they created massive inequality. The market distributes rewards in a skewed manner. The outcome was what Will Hutton calls the 30–30–40 society with a bottom 30 per cent on low wages or welfare benefits and dependent upon deteriorating public services, a middle 30 per cent with semi-detached houses and comfortable incomes along with a growing unease about job security and a top 40 per cent with high earnings, large homes and private pensions and health schemes (1995). Frequently, the bottom 30 per cent are located in council estates. Indeed, nearly half of all council tenant households have no earner (Joseph Rowntree Foundation, 1996).

Thirdly, New Right proponents engendered a morality which tolerates massive poverty in the midst of affluence. Ours is a society in which it is not considered wrong for some families to possess two homes and enjoy holidays abroad while fellow citizens rent a damp, overcrowded flat and never go on holiday. It is a morality, or immorality, which has pervaded all institutions with, for example, New Labour cabinet ministers taking £100,000 a year and welfare directors taking £70,000 while overseeing services which are supposed to help the poor. Such is individualism. But, as Vernon White, the Chancellor of Lincoln Cathedral, points out in his scholarly review, *The New Right*, emphasis is not really about liberal individualism, it is about egoism in which individuals manipulate others for their own ends (1996). Unfortunately, the dawn of a new government in Britain in 1997 has not seriously challenged this immorality. For instance, the government is to pay £9 million in fees to one agency to raise money for the Millennium Dome in London – itself a disgraceful expression of lavishing £500 million where it is not needed.

Fourthly, not content with escalating inequalities, the New Right gurus put the blame for poverty on the poor. Single mothers are demonised for having children on the state. Oddly enough, their arrows are aimed only at low-income parents not at aristocratic women who breed outside of marriage and certainly not at MPs who participate in the breeding. Much poverty and unemployment is attributed to an underclass made up, according to Charles Murray, of barbaric youths who refuse to work and then steal to get drugs and of immoral girls who want children without the nuisance of a man to act as father. The young women then raise more uncontrollable kids who will not work when they are adults. Murray cites Easterhouse as a classic example of a domain of the underclass, one of those 'communities without fathers [where] the kids tend to run wild' (1990: 12). The deduction made from this analysis is that the poor must be persuaded to leave poverty by withdrawing their state benefits. This philosophy has been softened but not removed by New Labour. The assumption behind this Government's new Welfare to Work programme is that there are thousands of young people who refuse to work and whose benefits must be cut to make them take up jobs.

Poverty pre-dated the New Right. But the latter's policies and philosophies have increased poverty and inequality and made Britain a more divided, less cohesive society. Simultaneously, local government services to low-income residents have been subject to severe restraints. The adverse effects have been most severely felt in the inner cities and council estates. Hence certain neighbourhoods have become more deprived. The plight of some has become desperate.

Examples of deprived neighbourhoods

Let me give two examples of contemporary deprived neighbourhoods. One from East London, which I knew as a child, and one from Glasgow where I now live. The Kingsmead Estate, not far from Hackney Marshes in London, and with a population of approximately 3,000, has the largest number of football pitches in Europe. As a youngster I spent hours not so much playing football there but looking for our pitch. The dwellings are mainly in blocks of flats. Initially, they were respected, sought after, working class residences. Not now. Roger Green, in conjunction with residents, has written an account of the estate. They describe the environment in these words:

> The physical decay of the estate is obvious. Some of the exterior walls of the blocks are running with water. Many have damp patches ... electrical cables and other assorted wiring hang limply from the walls (1997: 34).

Over half the residents are dependent upon earnings or benefits at Income Support levels. Forty-seven per cent of tenants are in rent arrears at an average of £1,000 per householder. Local services are considered poor and elderly members express fear.

Easterhouse is a huge housing scheme on the edge of Glasgow with a population of around 40,000. Extensive housing improvements are taking place under the local authority, housing associations and housing co-operatives. Yet many families still remain badly housed. Furthermore, 81 per cent of school children qualify for school clothing grants, that is they come from families with very low incomes. Of 25,000 eligible adults, only 8,500 are in full-time jobs. Long-term unemployment amongst the young can push some of them into finding outlets in crime and drug abuse. For example, a boy came into our office one day and emptied a plastic bag which contained 51 needles, all picked up in his tenement close. At 8.30 one morning, a car drew up outside our project and a man was flung out who had been knee-capped, probably for debts related to drugs. These deprivations are not the whole picture. But they exist and are typical of what is happening on thousands of other deprived neighbourhood estates.

The combination of escalating inequality and the deterioration of essential social services means that social exclusion is a characteristic of the lives of many residents of such neighbourhoods.

They are excluded from the *physical safety* which is accorded to the affluent. Children in Social Class V are 16 times more likely than those in Social Class I to die from house fires. They are more liable to road accidents, illnesses and death. Overcrowded and damp homes, lack of gardens and inadequate nutrition all take their toll.

They are excluded from the *family security* known to others. Children accommodated by public authorities are now overwhelmingly the children of the poor. As Bebbington and Miles (1989) concluded from their large-scale study, a child whose family is not on income support, is in a two-parent family with three or fewer children, is white, and lives in a spacious, owner-occupied house, has only a 1 in 7,000 chance of entering care. A child from a large, one-parent family, living on income support, of mixed ethnic origin, and dwelling in a crowded, privately rented home, has a 1 in 10 chance.

This is not to say that the children of most poor parents go into care. It is to say that social deprivations make parenting much harder which, in time, can adversely affect the children. Just over the road from our flat is a family where both parents work 72 hours a week at £2 an hour: their long hours and low pay does not make it easy to look after their five children.

They are excluded from *amenities*. Youngsters from comfortable backgrounds have the money to travel to and can afford recreation and facilities. Those in deprived neighbourhoods have little money and few facilities. I have been encouraging a few people in Easterhouse to write. One mother with four children wrote: 'Easterhouse is not an easy place for teenagers. The Sports Centre is quite expensive and it is in the centre where a lot of kids will not go in case they get jumped.' After her teenager daughter was sexually assaulted, she is frightened to let her go out.

They are excluded from *jobs*. A youngster wrote:

> I went on a job training scheme doing community industry and then catering. That was a year and a half ago and I have been on the broo [unemployment benefit] since then. I have been trying to get jobs but they keep on saying there are no vacancies or we will get in touch – but I never hear.

They are excluded from the *good life* enjoyed by so many in our society. Recently a young mother came to my flat. Aged 19, she looked undernourished and ill. One of her three kids spotted a banana, asked for it and quickly scoffed it. She was in debt, the washing machine was broken, she was fed up with protecting the kids from the needles on the stairs. She never goes out. She sobbed, 'I can't carry on any longer'. Compare that with those families who can spend more on one meal than she gets in a week, whose kids are well-dressed and are driven to stimulating recreations. She is excluded from the good life, she can not move, the future looks bleak.

The neighbourhood response

Interestingly, the concept of neighbourhood or community now appears to be regaining some popularity. Within social work, a small number of practitioners never lost the faith and BASW now has a Special Interest Group in Community Social Work. Academically, Amitai Etzioni preaches the virtues of communitarianism (1997) and is said to have influenced senior British politicians who, before the last election, began to claim that strong neighbourhoods were the counter to crime and vandalism. Post-election, this has not resulted in any concrete help for the neighbourhoods and it was noticeable that the term community did not appear in the Queen's Speech at the start of the new government in 1997.

But there is a response to neighbourhood deprivation. It is coming not from outside but from inside the localities. I am referring to neighbourhood groups which I define as 'the residents of a small locality acting together in projects for the collective well-being of members and their neighbourhood' (Holman, 1997: 103). In his report *Social Inclusion and Citizenship in Europe,* Paul Henderson explains that community development (which embraces neighbourhood groups) is growing throughout Europe. He provides case studies of local job creation schemes, pensioner clubs, community associations, housing co-ops, public forums, etc. in Sweden, Hungary, Spain and the Netherlands (1997). In Britain, the Community Development Foundation estimates that around 2.5 million people are involved in local voluntary groups which organise credit unions, youth clubs, play schemes, community transport, welfare rights projects, day care centres and so on.

FARE

As an example of a neighbourhood group, I will talk about the one I have been associated with in Easterhouse. Called FARE (Family Action in Rogerfield & Easterhouse), it was established in 1989 with the objective of 'promoting the welfare of the inhabitants of Easterhouse, especially the neighbourhood of Rogerfield'. Its committee members are elected at an AGM and consist of people from the area, that is from people who know what it is like at the hard end. Funds have come mainly from voluntary sources. FARE has operated from a small office and had one and a half staff. I was the half. Following a financial crisis, I became a volunteer. However, FARE has recovered and now has three staff and has recently moved into its own premises, five hard-to-let flats – hard-to-let because a number of drugs deaths occurred in them.

What does FARE do?

FARE runs extensive youth facilities. Clubs have been held in two schools at lunch times and evenings with over 300 children participating each week. The minibus is used for swimming, skating, bowling trips. In the summer, holidays are arranged for 150 youngsters. FARE participates in community activities. Its members were involved in the establishment of a credit union which has flourished and a food co-op which has floundered – mainly due to repeated break-ins. They help with a local paper. FARE owns a caravan, for which two committee members take responsibility, which is fully booked from April to September and provides cheap holidays at the seaside. The Group gives support to some vulnerable families and individuals. Staff and volunteers help families fill in social security applications – like over 100 questions in the three books of forms for disability and incapacity benefit. They may accompany families to Children's Hearings, to meetings with social workers, to negotiations with housing officials. In a three year period we recorded the reasons why 65 callers came to our flat on 757 occasions. The main reason in two thirds of the cases was a lack of money – people in debt, wanting a second hand cooker, asking for a loan for a power card, penniless until the next giro comes. One boy came to us and said, 'Mum says can you lend her two tea bags?'

Contributions
FARE has had limitations and failures: it has failed to engage some residents, failed to reach some young people, has alienated some families. But it has made some contributions to the neighbourhood.

For a start, youth clubs, trips and holidays are now established in a district where there had been little provision. The clubs might be deemed old fashioned – table tennis, board games, craft – but they do draw large numbers of children. In our area, youngsters spend much time on the streets. This can be healthy as they interact and play traditional games. But there are also dangers if they get drawn into vandalism, drinking, gang fights and the ever available drugs. In the summer evenings, several gang fights occur. Police intervention is ineffective. Parents know that, at least in the clubs, their children are safe. The clubs can be an alternative to the excesses of gang life. The clubs also provide a meeting place where staff and volunteers relate with youngsters. These contacts then prove the basis for a closer relationship with a few, more needy members.

Let me give an example of what I call resourceful friendship. Brian, aged nine, joined the clubs where he displayed much aggression. He was from a large, very poor family and, with his mum's permission, I gave him a great deal of time. I taught him table tennis, swimming and other sports. At secondary school, his disruptive behaviour led to exclusion and expulsion. The same happened at another school and he had no further school education. My aim became just to keep him off drugs and out of custody until he was 16. We succeeded. He is now 17, has had much unemployment and prospects are not good. But it is not just youngsters. Places like Easterhouse have many inhabitants who want to improve their neighbourhood. Neighbourhood groups like FARE offer the opportunities. Since its inception, FARE has involved over 100 local people as committee members and volunteers. Some drift away, others last. Most get satisfaction in helping out. For others, it has a more profound effect. Cindy was a lone parent who had suffered traumatic childhood experiences. She had two short-lived marriages and other unsatisfactory relationships. She loved her daughter but had difficulties. Eventually she agreed to her daughter going into care for a short period. Then access was reduced and eventually social workers told her that they were applying for the daughter to be 'freed for adoption'. Cindy was devastated and turned to FARE for help. After long negotiations with Children's Hearings and courts, she was restored to her. Interestingly, Cindy had become involved with the Food Co-op, indeed was elected its chairperson. She said it was the first time she was accorded respect and it had a positive effect on her self-esteem. I must add that, more importantly, she had married a stable and loving husband who was accepting of her daughter. None-the-less, the recognition she received in the co-op did give her some confidence which, I think, was carried over into her relationships at home.

If FARE has made any contribution I think it stems from two factors. One is that the project is rooted in the neighbourhood. It runs numerous youth activities because this is what residents have requested. Furthermore, volunteers and sessional staff are locals. One parent showed his commitment and skills for seven years as a volunteer. He is now a full-time member of staff. He knows the dynamics of the area, he can handle the teenagers, many of whom he has known since they were babies, and he is not easily conned. The other factor is that FARE is long-term. Its staff and helpers do not stay a couple of years and go. They have a commitment to the neighbourhood. This means that they see families in the good times as well as the bad, observe their strengths as well as their weaknesses. And it means that they win trust.

The importance of neighbourhood groups

FARE is just one of thousands of neighbourhood projects. Having visited many and having read about many more, I believe that they are of importance for the following reasons:

They strengthen neighbourhoods

For all their limitations, neighbourhood groups have established a whole variety of local services which would not otherwise exist. They have drawn in resources, improved the environment, encouraged local volunteers, created a more positive image of their area and its people. In short, they facilitate the self-help and the readiness to help each other which is the essence of the good neighbourhood. They thus counter some of the forces which have been undermining neighbourhoods in the post-war period.

They are preventative

Neighbourhood groups tend to offer the kind of services which people want. Cheap credit, moderately priced food, holidays, day care, youth activities. They are available with no sense of stigma because residents choose to go to them and because the projects have no powers to remove children or prosecute parents. They cannot eradicate the poverty suffered by many residents but they can alleviate some of its effects. These practical services can both divert youngsters from destructive activities and help mothers and fathers cope with parenting. Hence they are essentially preventative. Anne Power and Rebecca Tunstall investigated violent disturbances in 13 areas in the UK. Amongst their main recommendations to avoid such riots was 'more support for residents' groups and for those seeking to improve life on estates' (1997). In her study of prevention,

Jane Gibbons concluded, 'parents under stress more easily overcome family problems...when there are many sources of family support available in local communities' (Gibbons et al., 1990: 162).

They offer a different kind of service
Statutory social services with powers to intervene and professional social workers skilled in assessment are important services. But they operate on a long established model in which experts from outside are sent in to deal with families who are deemed inadequate. Not surprisingly, the controlling and stigmatising elements of this approach often have a negative effect on the recipients. Neighbourhood groups can offer a different kind of service, one which may even forestall statutory action. It is a service from staff or volunteers who probably do not hold professional qualifications but who do live in the area and who do come from similar background to users. The model is one in which help comes from within the neighbourhood and in which the help is conveyed in a positive fashion.

This kind of work has been studied in Australia by Jane Thomson who, in her PhD, compares statutory welfare staff with the unqualified workers in a voluntary, community project who were engaging with parents with multiple problems. The professionals had definite skills and wide knowledge. Yet, in many ways, the unqualified local staff got closer to users because they had been through similar difficulties. Moreover, they were not regarded as threats but rather as what Thomson calls 'mentors', who gave encouragement and acted as role models. They conveyed positive messages to the parents which enabled them to set realistic targets for themselves which, when attained, improved their self-confidence and their handling of family relationships. Simultaneously, the community project was regarded as a kind of bolt-hole to which users could turn at times of crisis. Thomson concluded that the key element possessed by the local staff was that they had a style which tended 'to break down the hierarchy of authority and control which operates in relation to workers in social welfare' (1997: 300).

Thomson's analysis is similar to a less academic one which I made of staff in voluntary neighbourhood centres (Holman, 1988b). It holds for some full-time staff in neighbourhood projects. It is a supportive service which emphasises the strengths not the weaknesses of users. In a small way it counters the feelings of powerlessness and hopelessness imposed on victims by an unequal society.

They challenge the notion of an underclass
Of course, deprived neighbourhoods do contain criminals, drug abusers and those who pursue sex outside of stable relationships. But then so does parliament and the City of London. The point is that the deprived neighbourhoods are not a dominant army which is breeding so fast as to turn whole estates into barracks of the underclass. Deprived neighbourhoods are much more characterised by decent families who dislike crime and drugs and want the best for their children and communities. Many – including unemployed people and single parents – contribute to neighbourhood groups. They act responsibly, they live stable lives, they are not an underclass. Nonetheless, many still remain poor and unemployed.

In other words, their social deprivations spring not from their personal and moral inadequacies but rather from the economic and social circumstances in which they are forced to live.

They express significant values

Not least, the values displayed by neighbourhood groups often stand in opposition to the egoism, the greed and the selfishness which have almost become virtues. Neighbourhood groups show that practical services can be provided by co-operation rather than competition. They are made possible by members who, far from receiving personal, material gain, make sacrifices in order to serve others. Of course, participants gain satisfaction and self-esteem but this is achieved by benefiting not exploiting the community. Neighbourhood groups are essentially mutual. Members accept obligations towards others in the expectation that others will co-operate with them in building a neighbourhood which is better for all.

In terms of shaping social and economic life, neighbourhood groups are dwarfs compared with governments, private enterprise and middle class think tanks. Yet they do engage with the structural causes of inequality and poverty in this way. Ultimately all policies spring from values. Neighbourhood groups give expression to beliefs in co-operation, mutuality, equality, which must become widespread if income, wealth and power are ever to be re-distributed. Their voice is a whisper but the hope must be that – in conjunction with others such as that of some churches – the whisper from the bottom eventually overtakes those who can shout at the top.

I dream. Meanwhile, neighbourhood groups are acting in ways which are inclusive not exclusive. They include in action and responsibility people who have been marginalised by current forces. They include as participants those whom statutory services treat as recipients. In credit unions, food co-ops, housing co-operatives and so on, they include citizens who have hitherto been excluded from influence in the markets of credit, food and housing. As Paul Henderson says of community development which, in his terms, embraces neighbourhood groups:

> Inclusion gives a message of people joining in activities, debates and decision making, not of being shut out. Community development is committed to participation, not in a loose, generalised way but in the sense of enabling people who have little or no experience of participation, or who are disillusioned with what they have experienced, to become involved in a genuine civil society (1997: 9).

The future of neighbourhood groups

Neighbourhood groups promote social inclusion. They challenge the forces which undermine neighbourhood. Ironically, just as their contribution is being recognised so their financial position, never strong at the best of times, is becoming weaker. Central government will make grants to the national voluntary societies but tells neighbourhood groups to apply to their local authorities. But local authorities, never generous towards local groups, have less to distribute for two reasons. One is that, in the era of the contract culture, they favour the financially sound and larger voluntaries who can deliver services which are really statutory requirements. The other is that central government financing of local authorities has often pushed the latter into making cuts with their axe then failing on small voluntary groups. Glasgow is a prime example. In the shake-up of local government in Scotland, the huge region of Strathclyde was abolished while Glasgow became a unitary authority but one bereft of the richer suburbs and left with four huge deprived estates. The outcome has been enormous cutbacks. Des McNulty, a senior councillor, points out that the cuts:

> target more clearly on some of the weakest and most vulnerable communities and groups in the city. The total budget for voluntary sector projects aimed at needy groups, which in the past for Glasgow would have amounted to £8–9 million over the next three years, has been slashed to just £2.1 million – a cut of 76 per cent (1997).

Easterhouse possessed the city's busiest community centre, home to 26 local groups. It was closed along with scores of other projects. FARE receives not a penny from the local authority towards the salaries of its staff. It has to pay the full rent for the hard-to-let flats which have become its base. Neighbourhood groups turn to the National Lottery, which, whilst being able to find £18 million for the Tate Gallery and £7million for a new cricket ground for Hampshire Cricket Club, has no strategy for reviving deprived neighbourhoods. The neighbourhood groups approach the charitable trusts, many of whom are sympathetic towards deprived areas but who are overwhelmed with applications. Residents in the inner cities and peripheral estates are willing to give their time, skills and commitment towards improving their neighbourhoods, but they cannot be expected to provide the cash. This has to come from outside.

Elsewhere I have put forward a proposal to secure stable funding for neighbourhood groups. It is that the government should finance a National Neighbourhood Fund (Holman, 1997). It would allocate money to 250 community trusts covering the 250 most deprived areas in Britain. The members of the trusts would be elected from their areas. They would distribute money to locally run groups. If adequate, regular funding were available to neighbourhood groups, these outcomes could be anticipated:

- democracy would be advanced. Citizens who are usually excluded from power would be represented on boards which distribute resources while more would participate in local groups;
- local services would be extended so raising the quality of life for those in the bottom 30 per cent;
- vibrant services which reflect what people want would make for stronger, more cohesive neighbourhoods;
- local employment would increase as credit unions, food co-ops and youth projects, for example, recruited more staff from their areas. In places like

Easterhouse there are already several hundred good jobs and salaries. They go to teachers, social workers, doctors and local authority officials who mainly live outside the area and so spend their incomes elsewhere. By emphasising local recruitment, neighbourhood groups would ensure that more money is invested where it is most required. Deprived neighbourhoods would again have jobs.

If each appointed community trust received an annual £3million the total cost would be £750 million a year. No doubt, the objection will be made that 'the nation cannot afford such expenditure'. Nonsense. Britain is an affluent country. It possesses over 95,000 millionaires. In 1993–94, government departments lavished £865 million on outside management consultants. Personally, I wish to see not just a minimum wage but a maximum one for I see no reason why anyone needs an income of over £30,000 a year. It is not a matter of whether government can afford to revive deprived areas but whether it is willing to do so.

CHAPTER 7

Exclusion: The Emperor's Clothes

Bill Fisher

This chapter explores the topic of social exclusion with particular reference to disabled people. It suggests that, although we are all familiar with physical and social exclusion whether on the grounds of gender, 'race', sexual orientation or any other factor, to understand the physical and social exclusion experienced by disabled people, we need to look at some of the major components which influence everyone's life and to assess whether each of them represents no influence on the individual, has an adverse influence, or presents few difficulties.

Figure 1 lists the components of life where people without an impairment and people with an impairment will experience different effects. This is by no means an exhaustive list but it identifies some of the major components of life and

Figure 1: Components of life

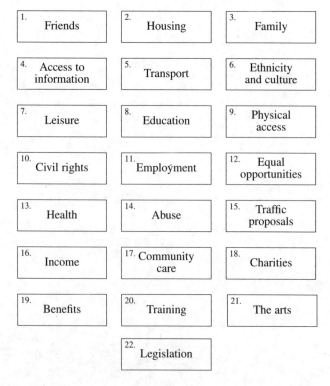

1. Friends	2. Housing	3. Family
4. Access to information	5. Transport	6. Ethnicity and culture
7. Leisure	8. Education	9. Physical access
10. Civil rights	11. Employment	12. Equal opportunities
13. Health	14. Abuse	15. Traffic proposals
16. Income	17. Community care	18. Charities
19. Benefits	20. Training	21. The arts
22. Legislation		

Source: Fisher 1997

74

allows an element of discussion on how these components influence physical and social exclusion in the lives of disabled people when compared to non-disabled people. I recognise that subjectivity has a strong influence on all that I have to say. However, I believe earnestly that life experience (subjectivity redefined) is a sensitive and accurate informer of our society today.

Figure 2 depicts the degree of influence or effect of these components of life on a person without an impairment. I would suggest that those that have little or no influence in excluding a person without an impairment from our society are charities, equipment and community care.

Charities were established in the dim and distant past to try, among other things, to redress the imbalance of social exclusion experienced by identifiable sectors of our society. In the course of day to day living, many charities do not feature in the lives of people without impairments. At the lowest level of involvement they may give a donation to the charity and at the highest level of involvement they may give voluntary service to the charity. However, such involvement has no direct influence to exclude them socially. Indeed, the

Figure 2: Components of life
Person without an impariment

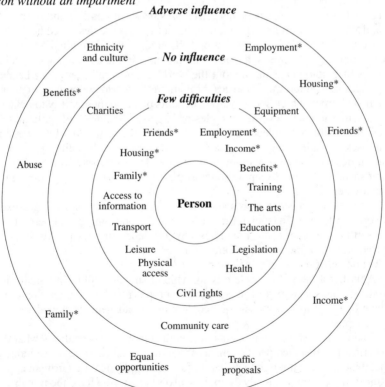

*indicates variable nature of influence
Source: Fisher 1997

opposite may be true, because involvement with a charity is seen as being laudable and can be an aid to social inclusion in certain sectors of our society.

Equipment is a very broad term but, in the context of social exclusion it includes items which are essential to aid a particular facet of life, for example a computer with speech synthesizer software to enable a person with a visual impairment to access printed information. There are few examples of equipment needed by a person without an impairment to reduce social exclusion.

Community care is the social system in the UK which purports to enable marginalised people to live in the community instead of being confined to an existence in institutions. This component of life has no direct influence on people without impairments.

Components like leisure, transport and the arts generally present few difficulties for a person without an impairment and do not contribute to social exclusion. Rather than discussing the detail at this point, I will describe how these components of life influence social exclusion of people with impairments later in this chapter.

Income, benefits, housing, friends, family and employment are the components of life which have the greatest variation in how they affect social exclusion. They can present either few difficulties or exert an adverse influence on social inclusion. Interpersonal difficulties between families and friends are so manifold and so well known that they do not need to be described here.

Housing, when in poor condition, unsuited to the individual or located on peripheral estates, exerts a particular adverse influence on social inclusion. Levels of employment throughout the world are generally dropping because of advances in technology. Countries throughout the world are now recognising the financial burden which social welfare benefits place on their ability to balance the books and there are several examples of large scale reviews of particular social welfare benefits or, indeed, the entire social welfare system. However, for the purposes of this chapter, a snapshot indicates that benefits represent few difficulties for a person without an impairment or exercise adverse influence on their social inclusion, except in so far as they may be a disincentive to taking paid employment.

Even as we speed towards the millennium, ethnicity and culture exert an adverse influence on social inclusion. Equal opportunities are espoused but converting the theory into practice seems to elude our society. Abuse, whether verbal, physical, racial, sexual, emotional or cultural, is still the greatest adverse effect on achieving social inclusion.

A further aspect of everyday living which I suggest will have a major impact on increasing social exclusion is the traffic proposals which the UK is promoting. The effect of traffic proposals on people with impairments is considered later in this chapter.

Taking these same components of life, the chapter next analyses what the life experience of disabled people tells us about the influence of these components on social inclusion. Although this chapter focuses on physical impairment and social exclusion, much of the analysis applies also to those who have the impairment of unemployment, homelessness, etc.

I recognise that I could be accused of exaggerating the situation but I shall explain why I have placed each of the components on the sociogram in Figure 3.

Friends and family are the most variable of the components. There is evidence to suggest that they can present few difficulties, exert no influence, or exert adverse influence. The family can qualify for entry in each of the categories in Figure 3. The family can be supportive or destructive or both at the same time. Independence for anyone is a difficult objective to achieve. However, when disability is added there can often be a mismatch between good intention and effect. We all acknowledge that young adults will leave the family home and this generates anxiety particularly for parents. Generally, young adults make a stable transfer to independent living with parental agreement. However, there are cases of disabled young adults wishing to take up independent living where parental

Figure 3: Components of life
Person with an impariment

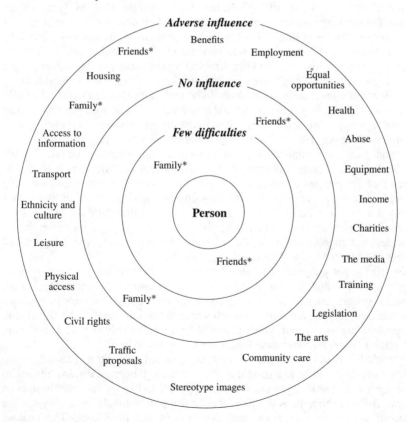

*indicates variable nature of influence
Source: Fisher 1997

reaction is, to say the least, negative. The natural parental concerns about how their children will cope with living outside the family home are amplified beyond reasonable measure. There is acknowledgement that disabled young adults should be allowed to take the same level of risk as their non-disabled peers. The irony is that in all such cases I have witnessed, disabled young adults have the same successes and failures as anyone else.

Friendship is an integral part of human experience. It gives us the confidence to explore our personalities and to develop our personal functions. To develop interpersonal skills, humans need to be able to communicate, congregate and interact. However, whilst people without impairments may have difficulty with each of these actions, the dislocation they experience is much less than that usually experienced by disabled people. All of the components of life on the sociogram contribute to increased dislocation experienced by disabled people.

Housing is another central facet of each of our lives. Without it we have no safe havens in which to plot our future. Why then do we continue to build houses which are designed to meet the needs of the average 5' 8" right-handed man? Probably because the world of architecture is dominated by men. What reasonable thinking woman would insist that standard designs for houses should have steps to the front door? She knows that pushchairs are not easy things to haul up steps. She knows that standard narrow door entries are difficult to negotiate. What reasonable thinking disabled person would design a house with steps, light switches at high levels, electric sockets at floor level, central heating controls at floor level and narrow doors? The real sadness is that disabled people have been highlighting these issues for many years. But it does not appear that the message is getting across to those with the power to bring about change. For example, Scottish Homes, the government's strategic housing agency in Scotland, has just completed a consultation on design guides for housing for disabled people (Scottish Homes, 1996). Within that consultation, it is clearly stated that if a ramped entrance to a house is provided then it is mandatory also to provide steps. And here is the rub, if steps are provided at the entrance to a house, it is not mandatory to provide a ramp. I accept that there are factors such as ground levels on sites which may militate against ramped entrances being provided, but much more could be achieved if the principle was adopted and exceptions granted to meet particular circumstances.

Seventy eight per cent of disabled people rely on benefits for their income. While an individual may well qualify for a number of benefits, the British benefits system creates and maintains a poverty trap. Disabled people are marginalised because coming off benefits to enter employment will bring an end to certain benefits without which it would be very difficult to live. There is no incentive to enter employment. The poverty trap is too tight.

Health for disabled people is used as a mixed metaphor. The prevailing attitude is that if you have a disability you are immediately unhealthy. Yet health techniques are used to try to assist disabled people to live the life they have been given. The real problem with this is that health professionals invariably see the issue of health as a problem that lives within the individual. The process employed to deal with that problem is rehabilitation. In other words assisting the disabled person to learn to live with their disability. However, in relation to disability the process of rehabilitation exists in a vacuum. There is no element within rehabilitation which reflects the socio-economic reality of the world in which we live. Unless we, as a society, recognise the barriers we create which engender social exclusion and adjust practices in a wide range of disciplines to address those barriers, we will perpetuate the social exclusion of disabled people.

The cost of equipment to enable disabled people to interact with society can be high, especially when so many disabled people rely on benefits for their income. For example, a computer with speech synthesizer to assist visually impaired people costs £1500 – compare that with the cost of a pen for sighted people. A lightweight wheelchair will cost upwards of £1200 – compare that with the cost of a pair of shoes for an ambulant person.

Income, whether sourced by benefits or paid employment, is a precious commodity. But the demands on the income of disabled people are much more strenuous and wide ranging than for non-disabled people. The simple act of going to a cinema is fraught with additional expense; because of a variety of mobility restrictions the disabled person usually will be unable to use the public transport system others take so much for granted. Specialised transport is underprovided and even if available is more expensive than public transport. The only viable alternative is private transport such as taxis with the additional expense. There is, of course, an assumption here that all taxis are accessible but in most parts of our society that is not the norm.

Transport is a major issue. The Department of the Environment has recently launched a consultation paper entitled *Developing an Integrated Transport Policy* (1997) because it recognises the need to reduce pollution and congestion caused by personal use of the motor car. The proposal is that citizens should make more use of public transport, and that there should be more pedestrianised areas and a variety of other measures to exclude private cars from densely populated areas. The irony is that disabled people have been pressing for an integrated transport system for decades – an accessible system which everyone can use. However, the consultation does not propose accessible transport. These proposals can only lead to further social exclusion of disabled people. Lack of accessible public transport and road pricing – paying a toll to use certain roads or to drive in cities – will place excessive financial strain on disabled people and exacerbate the social exclusion they experience.

Every society or sector of society has its pecking order. It is hard to justify but it does exist. Within the disability world there is a clear recognition that a black or ethnic minority disabled woman who is a lesbian with children is likely to be the lowest on that pecking order. The disability movement is aware of this and, at least, tries to address these issues. The real tragedy is that we as a society have developed so many labels which can create and maintain social exclusion.

Physical access and access to information are the gatekeepers. These are the components of life which can create and maintain social exclusion or social inclusion. In simple terms, if you do not know about a function or a service how can you interact with it? Similarly if you cannot physically access a function or service how can you interact with it? The reality of our society is that it is the socially excluded who are expected to bring about change by representation or advocacy. But there are sound economic reasons why those in our society without disabilities should make the necessary changes to physical access and access to information. Recent research in the UK shows that the annual spending power of disabled people and their families is £31bn. In the European Union, the equivalent annual spending power is £200bn.

Stereotype images exercise great influence and contribute significantly to social exclusion. They do not relate exclusively to disability but they can and do influence public thinking. There is the recurring debate about the supermodels of the fashion industry. It is assumed that their slimness creates the epitome of the beautiful woman. Yet, many representatives of the women's movement are questioning the validity of this portrayal. They question the effect it has on women who, in comparison, could be described as slightly or even greatly overweight. I understand and support this challenge to stereotype images. But, let us pause for a moment – if non-disabled women are questioning the value of this portrayal and the effect the promotion of the body beautiful has on them, how much greater an adverse effect does it exercise in the perception of women with disabilities? Equally, think of how disabled people are portrayed by the media. How often can you recall a report which was not styled either on the basis of unfortunates to be pitied or of brave but tragic people.

The arts, and for convenience I will include advertising here, perpetuate the stereotypes. Twentieth century arts have their highest profile in the vehicle of cinema. Let us take the very popular series of Batman films and acknowledge that every villain in those films had a disability – most often facial disfigurement. These films are aimed at a young audience and I submit that the subliminal message that disability equals evil will add considerably to the factors which perpetuate social exclusion.

Advertising is no better. We only need to think of government campaigns to encourage us to drive more safely, reduce our speed or resist the temptation to drink and drive. Of course, as a society, we recognise that one of the consequences of bad driving can be death or damage to our bodies. Wide circulation of images of disabled people as being the ultimate unacceptable penalty for those actions may make people think about their own actions, but what a price disabled people are involuntarily forced to pay to get that message across.

Charities play a significant role in the processes of social exclusion and social inclusion. It is only in recent years that charities in the UK have been allowed to advertise to try to attract donations from the public. I regret to say that in relation to disability many charities have used offensive images in their advertising campaigns. I also have some concern about the asset base of charities. For example, charities in Scotland have an asset base of £4bn. When we exclude fixed assets such as buildings and land the remaining total assests and investments are £2.5bn (ONS, 1996). I recognise and accept that it is prudent to make financial provision for the future but I have to question whether retaining such large sums in investments is achieving the objectives for which these not for profit organisations have been set up.

Exclusion: the emperor's clothes

These are some of the components of life which perpetuate social exclusion in relation to disabled people. Let me now turn to what we as a society have done to try to convert social exclusion into social inclusion. Every civilised democratic society recognises the detrimental effects of social exclusion and promotes legislation which seeks to establish, in some cases, rights, and in other cases, social provision to reduce the effects of social exclusion. However, this is an opportune time to stop to examine such legislation to assess whether it resolves the difficulties it is designed to address; whether it is achieving the aims and objectives of social inclusion; and whether it is being undermined by current fiscal policies. In essence we must ask whether this legislation is effective or whether it merely aggravates social exclusion. I have here selected legislation relating to disability in the UK to illustrate the point. However, this type of scrutiny could be applied to any legislation in any country.

The first words of the Disability Discrimination Act (1995) are that it is 'an Act to make it unlawful to discriminate against disabled persons...'. Great, we say; disabled people will no longer have to suffer the social exclusion created by discrimination. But, sadly, this is not an accurate response. The Disability Discrimination Act introduces the novel concept that discrimination against disabled people can be justified. In effect, this means that any employer (with 20 or more employees) can convince himself or herself that although the disabled person is the best person for the job, a reason can be found to justify discriminating against that person and not giving him/her the job. Providers of goods and services (with any number of employees) can do the same to justify refusing to provide goods and services to disabled people on exactly the same basis as they would to any other member of the public. Prospective employers can use the cost of reasonable adjustments as a reason to justify discrimination against disabled people. The timescales for implementation of the goods and services provisions of this Act run up as far at the year 2012. Education and transport are exempt from these provisions of the Act.

A positive aspect of the employment provisions is that disabled people now have a right to ask an industrial tribunal to examine their claim that they have been discriminated against. But any application to an industrial tribunal has to be managed by the disabled individual with no formal support. Disabled people have no Commission similar to those established by sex and race legislation to assist managing cases and developing case law. The burden of pursuing claims of discrimination thus falls on the individual. Since 78 per cent of disabled people in the UK rely on benefits for their income and there is limited availability of legal aid, the number of cases being pursued will be greatly reduced.

It is informative to step back and look at the history behind the Disability Discrimination Act. Between 1985 and 1995 members of the opposition political parties in parliament responded to the representations made by disabled people about the need for civil rights legislation. It has to be emphasised that the opposition politicians with some members of the governing party did not only try once or twice to promote civil rights legislation. In a period of 10 years there were 14 attempts to create civil rights legislation. It is, therefore reasonable to expect that with such continuous pressure over a period of 10 years the end result would be encompassing and enabling legislation. However, disabled people in the UK are disappointed in the Disability Discrimination Act.

As mentioned earlier, the employment provisions of the Act apply only to employers who have 20 or more employees. Government figures confirm that 96 per cent of employers have fewer than 20 employees. Therefore, this legislation applies to only 4 per cent of employers in the UK. It is fair to say that many of the large employers have made efforts in recent years to look at how their policies and practices exclude disabled people from employment. I strongly believe that the employment provisions of the Act fail to achieve material, wide-ranging progress in the employment opportunities for disabled people.

Even with these massive limitations, the last government saw fit to include an all encompassing limitation in the Act. The Act says that discrimination against disabled people can be justified. I toyed with the idea of developing examples of justified discrimination in relation to gender and race. I have not done so, because there are no examples which would not be offensive. Justified discrimination is equally offensive to disabled people.

Goods and services are also covered by the Act. The first duties placed on providers are not to refuse service; not to provide service of a worse standard or in a worse manner; and not to provide service on less favourable terms. If disabled people consider that they have been discriminated against under any of those categories they can take the provider to court. Again, there is limited availability of legal aid to pursue a case and qualifying thresholds are set so low that many disabled people will not qualify for legal assistance.

So what happens if a case of this nature should go to court? If successful, the disabled person could receive compensation for any financial loss or injury to feelings. He or she may be able to get an interdict against the provider to prevent the repeat of any discriminatory act. But that interdict would apply only to that person – it does not extend automatically to other disabled people.

As the law stands at the moment the court can rule that there has been discrimination against a disabled person but it cannot rule that any adjustment should be made to ensure the discriminatory act is not repeated. Current government timetables suggest that this aspect will be brought into force in 2005 – 10 years after the Act was passed by parliament. My cynicism about government timescales will become more evident later in this chapter.

Transport and education get a fleeting mention in the Act, and the Act does not apply to buses or trains. At the moment there is no need to redesign buses and trains so that they are accessible to disabled people. Interestingly, however, our fair minded parliamentarians have written provisions affecting bus and train *stations*. The end result is that I as a disabled person can now enter bus and train stations which must be accessible and see all the pretty buses and trains which I cannot use. I have to say that this is a monument to the theory of inclusion!

The Act is incomplete and the theory is that successive governments will extend it by means of secondary legislation. There is currently consultation on the accessibility of taxis. The objective of the government is that all taxis should be accessible to disabled people by the year 2012: 17 years after the Act was passed by parliament. The government obviously wants to reduce social exclusion as quickly as possible!

The Act excludes education from the concept of unlawful discrimination that it promotes. Education establishments are not required to take steps to ensure that they do not discriminate against disabled people. Provision of education to disabled people relies on various Education Acts which say authorities have a duty to place disabled children in mainstream schools subject to the wishes of their parents and if the placement is appropriate to the child's needs; does not conflict with the needs of other children in the school; and is an efficient use of resources. This, in effect, perpetuates the special schools regime to provide education to disabled children.

In response to that provision of the Act, I can do no better than to quote Judith Huemann, Assistant Secretary of the US Office of Special Education and Rehabilitation in the United States. She suggests that 'those young people who are segregated in special schools will become adults who will continue to be segregated in life' (quoted in Lawrie, 1996: 13).

Education is the foundation on which people build to gain employment. The negative effect that these legal provisions for education will have on employment opportunities for disabled people is awesome.

Can legislation which claims to make it unlawful to discriminate against disabled people realistically reduce social exclusion when:

- discrimination against disabled people can be justified;
- the employment provisions apply only to employers with 20 or more employees when 96 per cent of employers have fewer than 20 employees;
- timescales for the implementation of the goods and services provisions run up to at least 17 years after the Act;
- there is no independent Commission to which disabled people can apply for legal support to pursue their claims;
- education and transport are exempt from the goods and services provisions of the Act.

The Chronically Sick and Disabled Persons Act (1970), for the first time, placed a duty on local authorities in the UK to make arrangements for promoting the welfare of disabled persons. (I must comment, in passing, on the title of this Act and how it reinforces the belief that disability equals illness). In effect, this Act is a needs-led provision. However, a recent case which went through the legal process and received a House of Lords ruling means that what was intended by the 1970 Act to be a needs-led provision is now a resources-constrained provision. The Lords reached this ruling by a 3 to 2 majority. I accept that there are arguments on each side but have to agree with Lord Lloyd who said:

> The solution lies with the government. The passing of the Chronically Sick and Disabled Persons Act 1970 was a noble aspiration. Having willed the end, parliament must be asked to provide the means (Lloyd, 1997).

In conclusion, this chapter has addressed some of the issues for those who are socially excluded by law as well as by practice. The fairy tales of Hans Christian Andersen include the tale of the Emperor's Clothes. Everyone was enthralled by the quality and style of the clothes until a child spoke the unthinkable – the Emperor was naked! The Emperor and everyone else had been duped into believing in the clothes. Should we now consider a similar examination of the legal fabric of our society lest we also have been duped?

CHAPTER 8

Social Exclusion and Social Work: Challenging the Contradictions of Exclusive Debate

Peter Beresford and Anne Wilson

The focus of this chapter is more the discussion about social exclusion and the composition and nature of that discussion, than social exclusion itself. Our particular concern is the perspectives of people identified as socially excluded and their actual and potential role in this debate. As psychiatric system survivors and workers in social work education, we both bring to this discussion two affiliations which relate to it in different ways. While we have strong views on this subject, complex issues are raised which should discourage any of us from coming to simplistic conclusions. Our aim is to encourage further thinking about the nature of this debate, particularly thinking which encourages tolerance, understanding and collaboration between us in our different, sometimes overlapping roles in the discussion.

The importance of the concept of social exclusion

We want to begin with social exclusion's new found importance in the UK. Social exclusion has developed rapidly in Britain, both as a conceptual and policy framework and a subject of study. It is now high both on research and political agendas. Social exclusion is now a major focus for social policy and social work research. Juliet Cheetham, who was a member of the social policy and social work panel, points out that in the 1996 UK Research Assessment Exercise a 'preoccupation with social exclusion was clearly apparent in ...submissions' (Cheetham, 1997). Why this interest? Clearly funding is forthcoming for it, with the interest in social exclusion of the European Union, Economic and Social Research Council and other funding organisations. Social exclusion offers researchers both a new framework for analysis and a new subject of analysis, particularly welcome at a time when traditional Fabian approaches to poverty and inequality have been facing both political and intellectual impasses.

The election of New Labour in 1997 has given social exclusion a new political significance in the UK. If the Conservative administration under Margaret Thatcher was seeking to abolish the word 'poverty', this Government seems set on replacing it with the term 'social exclusion'. Both welfare and anti-poverty policies are increasingly being framed in terms of social exclusion, both explicitly and implicitly. The most visible symbol of this development was the establishment of the government's Social Exclusion Unit in 1997.

We want next to try and say something about the meaning of social exclusion. First we should say that we do not have and do not intend to offer a definition of our own. That is not our aim here. It is clear that different meanings are attached to the term and that it is used in different ways. The term has its origins in a concern with inequality, restricted citizenship rights and poverty (Levitas, 1996: 7). It is still widely used to denote the same concern with disadvantage and oppression; the desire to challenge them and for people to participate fully socially, economically and politically and to be 'stakeholders' in society. We can expect to see the term increasingly used in this way by citizens', community and service users' organisations as its usage becomes more central in state policy and discussion. On this basis we may also see people who are researching and working with groups experiencing oppression, discrimination and disadvantage, or who are members of such groups themselves, coming together around this idea. For many of them, social exclusion may represent no more than an umbrella term, unifying and bringing them together and perhaps offering opportunities to identify common themes, share common problems and experience and explore alliances and common strategies and solutions.

Social exclusion and social control

But social exclusion has acquired other meanings. As Ruth Levitas says:

> The concept of social exclusion, which was originally developed to describe the manifold consequences of poverty and inequality…is now contrasted not with inclusion but with integration, construed as integration into the labour market…and treats social divisions which are endemic to capitalism as resulting from an abnormal breakdown in the social cohesion which should be maintained by the division of labour (Levitas, 1996: 5).

This approach to social exclusion reflects a concern with deviance and non-fulfilment of perceived obligations, both moral and economic and sees the solution to problems of social, family and personal breakdown and disruption in terms of assimilation into the labour market and social control. It serves to maintain and reinforce social divisions and inequalities rather than challenge them. It is this concept of social exclusion which is now the dominant one.

It is also this interpretation which is most closely reflected in present UK government philosophy and policy on social exclusion. This version of social exclusion is now one of a cluster of interrelated ideas to which New Labour has signed up, including 'communitarianism' and 'the underclass', which reflect a shift in ideology, a new concern with individual moral, social and economic responsibility and an emphasis on traditional values of family, nation, faith and work. Announcing the government's initiative on social exclusion, Peter Mandelson identified two groups. The first included disabled people, chronically sick and old people 'who we will continue to support'. The second was made up of 'others trapped by family background, mental illness, drug use', etc, where the aim is to get them 'out of these circumstances and into a normal life' (Mandelson, 1997a).

Ideas of 'underclass' and social exclusion both lump together a variety of disparate groups and phenomena for political, ideological and policy purposes. One difference between the two is that the emphasis of the 'underclass' is placed more specifically on groups perceived as dangerous and deviant. Social exclusion is used to include both those identified as dangerous and as unintentionally 'dependent', although as we can see from Peter Mandelson's comment, different responses are signalled, along traditional moral lines of 'deserving' and 'undeserving' (Mandelson, 1997b and 1997c). Furthermore, by framing policy in this way, (negative) ideas about groups who make up the category 'socially excluded' are likely to be transferable by association. In its first phase of work, the Social Exclusion Unit focused on three priorities; 'truancy and school exclusions', 'street living' and 'worst estates', suggesting it was working to a narrow and deviance-based conception of social exclusion (Social Exclusion Unit, 1997: 1).

This examination of social exclusion points to some more general observations. It is a problematic concept. We cannot take it for granted or simply attach our own meanings to it. It cannot be treated merely as a synonym or euphemism for poverty, inequality and disadvantage, as might be tempting for people unfamiliar with the debate. It is not an idea to be used naively or ingenuously. The concept is much more than the sum of the individuals and groups included within it. In any consideration of social exclusion, we must address the concept as well as those it is used to categorise. There are also some more specific concerns about its use. For example:

* being included in the category may have negative effects;
* the concept of social exclusion is not neutral, but has the potential to be harmful and regressive;
* regressive meanings now seem to be the dominant ones;
* uncritical acceptance of the idea and the assumption of shared, positive and progressive meanings, are likely to reinforce its regressive potential by strengthening its legitimacy and credibility.

The meanings which are attached to the term 'social exclusion' may become the lived realities of those who are included in its category. Ruth Levitas's analysis of the dominant discourse of social exclusion suggests that the discussion both generates and is founded upon the premise that the 'excluded' have already been discounted. They are not part of society. She points out that:

> The 'real' society is not that constituted by the (unequal) 70 per cent, to which the poor are marginal or from which they are excluded. The real society is that made up of the whole 100 per cent, in which poverty is endemic (1997: 19).

Debate which centres around the idea that people are not a part of society raises disturbing questions. It objectifies people who face exclusion, reducing them to 'material on which to work' (Goffman, 1975: 73). As well as being viewed as (passive) subjects of the debate, people included in the category may also become *objects* of that discussion.

We have looked at some of the competing meanings attached to the idea of social exclusion, but so far little has been heard about what those included under the heading think about it. One exception is the disabled people's movement where there is discussion of the social, economic and political exclusion which disabled people experience, as expressions of structural oppression, which is highlighted by the social model of disability (Oliver, 1990). While the idea of social exclusion does not originate from those labelled by it, we can expect them to have views about it, as they do about associated ideas of poverty, inequality, disability and so on.

So far those included in the category of social exclusion, have, however, played little if any part in the discussion about it and, as far as we know, have had few if any opportunities to take forward their own discussions of the idea. The category is administered and implemented by policy makers, professionals and academics, not 'excluded people'. The framework, subject matter and analyses of social exclusion all contribute to the definition, categorisation, classification and labelling of 'excluded people'. This serves to separate out and reinforce differences between 'experts' and those categorised as 'excluded'. While social exclusion has become a major focus of social work and social policy analysis, to the best of our knowledge, generally this has not extended to exploring the perspectives of 'the socially excluded' on the subject, nor to enable their analysis of the issue.

The UK Coalition Against Poverty, an alliance of over 150 organisations, including national charities and local community organisations, has called for people with experience of poverty to be consulted about the government's Social Exclusion Unit; to be represented among its members and for the Unit to be accessible and inclusive (Brighouse, 1997; Metz, 1997). While Frank Field, the Minister responsible for the reform of the welfare state, has expressed his interest in consulting claimants over benefit reform, so far no significant attempt has been made to do this (Field, 1997, personal communication). This reflects a much longer tradition of the non-involvement of welfare state service users in welfare debate and policy formation, which extends from the original establishment of the welfare state to the membership of the Commission on Social Justice and which embraces both major political parties (Croft and Beresford, 1993a; Beresford, 1995).

Exclusion from social work and social policy debates

The limited part people identified as socially excluded have played in social policy and social work analysis reflects a broader and more longstanding situation, which we and others have discussed in detail elsewhere (for example, Oliver, 1990, 1996; Beresford and Croft, 1995; Beresford, 1997; Beresford and Croft, 1997). The issue is now receiving increasing attention and some developments are taking place, particularly in social work, to include the perspectives of service users in its discussion and development, but there are still few coherent and systematic efforts to include the subjects of social policy and social work in its debate and their exclusion from it continues to be the rule rather than the exception.

The reasons for this remain unclear. Explanations which we and others have identified, particularly in relation to people with experience of poverty, disabled people and social care service users include:

- a tradition of professionals speaking for people, rather than conceiving of them as speaking for themselves;
- traditional models of analysis and campaigning based on evidence gathering by outside 'experts', seen as having credibility and legitimacy, seeking to 'educate the public';
- fears and anxieties about 'expert' professional and academic roles being threatened or undermined by the inclusion in debate of service users or the subjects of social policies;
- perceptions of people as unable to or uninterested in participating and concerns that participation would be 'too burdensome' for them, given the high levels of stress and hardship which many experience; and
- the ease of excluding them, since these groups generally lack the power to ensure their inclusion.

Social work discussion has not only largely excluded service users, it has also reinforced negative views of their capacity, generally viewing them in negative and deficit terms. As Chris Jones, the UK social work academic, points out:

> It is a somewhat sobering experience analysing social work education and its knowledge base. For, in its mainstream at least, historical exploration of the past 100 years reveals startling continuities, such as social work's construction of clients as generally unworthy and manipulative individuals. Such a construction has contributed to a tragic legacy whereby clients are too often disregarded, not listened to and generally presented as people who don't count. This in turn must contribute to the episodes of cruelty and inhumanity which are periodically exposed…One cannot but wonder about the impact of mainstream social work's construction of clients on this 'writing off' of vulnerable people (Jones, 1996: 197).

This in turn can only be expected to reinforce service users' exclusion from discussions that concern them, including those about social exclusion.

Exclusion: a particular problem for this discussion

The exclusion from debate of people on the receiving end of social work and social policy has special significance, and issues are raised with particular intensity in the context of discussion about social exclusion. First, it raises some central questions. Is there not an inherent contradiction here? If the aim is to address, indeed challenge, social exclusion, then is there not a fundamental problem if those included in the category are not fully included in discussion about it? Is it not essential to involve them in the process? If they are not represented in such discussion, does this not then mirror and reinforce the exclusion under discussion? Since the knowledges, viewpoints, analyses and interests of service users are likely to be different from those of others, does this not qualify the integrity and quality of discussion as well as mean that it loses important perspectives? How can such exclusive discussion be justified? It is difficult to see how questions can be asked and answers offered about social

90

90 *Social Exclusion*

exclusion unless all those concerned, including those included in the category themselves, have equal opportunities to contribute their perspectives, meanings and knowledges.

The second issue that is raised is the particularly harmful potential of the category social exclusion to those included in it. Fiona Williams has commented on the way in which the disabled people's and social care service users' movements:

> have grasped the administrative categories (or subject positions) imposed upon them by policy makers, administrators and practitioners and translated these into political identities and new subjectivities (Williams, 1996: 75).

Such administrative categories, like claimant, client, 'the poor', disabled, 'mentally ill', lone parents, 'learning disabilities' and so on, tend to be problematic for those to whom they are attached. They have generally been constructed without their involvement, re-interpreting their experience, imposing outside meanings on them and being associated with stigma. However the groups to whom they have been attached have shown that they can be reclaimed. The same is unlikely to be true of social exclusion. It, like other past and present generalist terms, including vagrancy, morally defective, residuum, lumpenproletariat, sociopath and 'underclass', has a particular capacity to harm because it combines a moral, ideological and policy purpose and can be attached arbitrarily to diverse individuals and groups.

The blanket (out)casting of people into excluded roles by social exclusion's academics and commentators bears a disquieting resemblance to what has gone before. For example, Race (1995: 48) cites Tredgold's ideas for dealing with the 'poor and handicapped sections of the population'. Tredgold advocated the prevention of 'propagation' and the protection of society from criminals and 'non-productive individuals' (Tredgold, 1909). In line with these eugenic ideals, the 1913 Mental Deficiency Act lumped together four disparate groups of 'defectives'; those classified as 'idiots', 'imbeciles', 'feebleminded persons' and 'moral defectives' and created mechanisms for their certification as 'fit persons to be removed' from society (Potts and Fido, 1991: 19). Most of those removed to the colonies and institutions of the time were excluded from society for decades of their lives. Others never returned. All were prevented from marrying or having (further) children for the duration of their incarceration (Ryan and Thomas, 1987; Potts and Fido, 1991; Barron, 1996).

Arguments for including people in discussion

Not only are there problems in excluding people from debate about social exclusion, there are also strong arguments in favour of involving people included in the category of social exclusion in the debate about it. Four central arguments emerge:

1. Better informed debate

The involvement of recipients of public policy in other fields has repeatedly been shown to improve its ability to promote their rights and meet their needs (Beresford and Croft, 1993). Their first hand knowledge and experience offers an invaluable basis for developing needs-led policy and practice. Debate about social exclusion can only be better informed if those directly affected are part of it. Their involvement makes it possible for the debate to identify, reflect and advance their needs, concerns and interests more accurately and closely and can enable more relevant and participatory research and analysis. In a context of restricted public resources, it can help make possible a more rational and democratic basis for priority setting.

2. Stronger and more effective action

Social policy and social work discussions and campaigns which have not involved the subjects of those discussions have had limited success. The lesson of recent politics is that popular discussions and campaigns are the ones which seem to make the most impact. We can see expressions of this new participatory politics in campaigns for disabled people's rights, the environment and against road building as well as in the black people's, gay men's and lesbian movements. Such campaigns mobilise large numbers of people, gain popular support and are not narrowly associated with a particular political or party interest. Such broad-based campaigns and their successes stand in contrast with narrowly-based welfare and anti-poverty campaigns.

3. Minimising the risks of 'objectification'

As we said earlier, there is a risk that social exclusion debate will work to *objectify* those under discussion. By including subjects in the debate, the risks of objectification and its consequences may be mitigated. At the level of service provision, objectification of service users has been proposed as a causal factor in the 'corruption of care' (Martin, 1984; Ryan and Thomas, 1987; Wardhaugh and Wilding, 1993):

> Once defined as less than fully persons, the way is clear to forms of behaviour and treatment which would be unacceptable with those not so stigmatised (Wardhaugh and Wilding, 1993: 27).

Objectification of 'excluded people' within social exclusion debate similarly leaves the way open for unacceptable treatment at a societal level. Debate which includes their voices is less likely to view its subjects as 'less than fully persons'.

4. Respecting the rights and citizenship of 'excluded' people

Including people in this discussion directly challenges the social exclusion with which it is concerned. It is part of the broader issue of addressing their restricted citizenship. It signifies respect for them, an acknowledgement that they have something to offer, that their contribution is important, worthwhile and valued, and recognition of their expertise in their own experience. The origins of the idea of social exclusion lie in redressing inequality. Supporting people to speak for themselves is a basic requirement for such equality. It makes it possible for them directly to challenge social exclusion and stereotypes of themselves as passive, lazy and incapable. This is especially important at a time of fundamental social, economic and political change, fed by 'globalisation', political realignments, electoral change and new technology. These are having a fundamental impact on all our lives, exposing people who were previously unaffected to new uncertainties and new risks and increasing the likelihood of people being identified as socially excluded.

Towards an inclusive debate

As can be seen, there are problems in excluding people who are included in the category of social exclusion from debate about it and strong arguments for including them. What then would an inclusive debate about social exclusion look like? We suggest that it would include three things:

- the *perspectives* of people identified as socially excluded, ensuring that all such groups were represented and reflecting differences of age, sexuality, gender, disability, 'race' and class;
- the *knowledges* of people identified as socially excluded. The groups included in the category have developed their own knowledges, based on their own experiences and understandings. These knowledges take different forms. Much is unwritten and unpublished. But groups are also writing their own accounts and histories (for example, Campbell, 1996; Campbell and Oliver, 1996; see also an initial bibliography by Beresford et al., 1997).
- the *analyses* of the subjects of social exclusion, including their interpretations, meanings, hypotheses and theories.

It is important that all three of these: perspectives, knowledges and analyses, are included in debate. It is not enough just to involve people to discuss their experience or give their views. This has been the traditional approach to participation in social care and poverty analysis and planning. It restricts the subjects of social work and social policy to being a data source to inform other people's analyses and conceptual frameworks. Control remains the same. This is a process of extraction rather than empowerment. It is essential instead that people included in the category social exclusion are enabled to develop their own analyses and to be part of the broader process of constructing knowledge and developing analysis and critiques.

These analyses may need to be developed away from dominant discussion and debate. It may prove difficult for 'excluded people' to formulate their own ideas or theories within a culture which works to maintain the dominant reality and to *resist change*. Given that the academic community plays a part in assigning them their 'excluded' status in the first place, 'excluded people's' contributions may well be resisted. Lena Dominelli (1997: 11) points out that mainstream academics whose views fall outside accepted paradigms may be labelled 'eccentric, pathological or socially inadequate'. It is not unlikely therefore that if the ideas of people identified as 'socially excluded' challenge accepted paradigms, they too will be similarly labelled, or their analyses viewed as symptomatic of some presumed pathology. The development of their own analyses may also entail people disaffirming their status as 'excluded people' and constructing an identity *for themselves*. They are unlikely to want or be able to do this within a debate where labelling agents, professionals and academics are also present.

Problems of inclusive debate

A powerful case therefore can be made for such an inclusive debate about social exclusion. But is inclusive debate necessarily a good thing? A number of key questions are raised here. While traditional discussants might have had their reasons for not including those associated with the concept in the discussion, there are also some major question marks for 'the socially excluded' themselves about getting drawn into the debate. Should we be encouraging subjects of social exclusion to contribute to it? Why should 'the excluded' want to take part in the debate and what gains and losses might there be for them? Will the debate be on their terms and in their forms? The lesson to be drawn from people's participation in user involvement discussions and initiatives in the social care service system is that little may be achieved for considerable effort (for example, Campbell, 1996; Beresford, 1997a). There is no guarantee that getting involved in this discussion will be any different. The energies and resources of individuals and groups might be diverted into a discussion which ultimately may not achieve much. Would people not be better off having their own debates based on their own conceptual frameworks, like, for example, disability and mental distress, rather than fitting into those of others?

Furthermore, if the subjects of such debate come to be included in it, is there likely to be any shift in control? Whose debate will it be? Will it still be dominated by the traditionally 'included', in terms of control, philosophy, funding and agendas? The issue of control is important in determining both collective and personal outcomes for those identified as 'socially excluded', influencing, for example, whether individuals are able to speak openly and say what they feel safely and without risk.

We should also ask whether, by taking part in and contributing to the construction of the idea of social exclusion, people will not reinforce and legitimate it and whether this could be damaging to them and their peers. In other words, if we contribute to the debate, do we become part of the problem? There are undoubtedly problems in participating in the development of an idea and category in which people may be included involuntarily and which reframes them and their experience, restructuring and misrepresenting both. As people potentially included in the category of social exclusion, we have asked ourselves whether we should be joining in this discussion at all and whether by adding our voices to and debating with it, we are not colluding with and reinforcing an inherently negative idea. On the other hand, if we do not contribute to the discussion, we may just give free rein to its most negative proponents? This is the Hobson's choice with which the subjects of social policy frequently find themselves faced.

There are other more specific issues that also need to be addressed. For example:

- is social exclusion a concept with which people and groups will wish to be associated? We know that some poor people do not want to be identified with poverty. (Lister and Beresford, 1991; Alcock, 1997) The same may be true of social exclusion; a similarly devalued and negative identity. Will everyone included in the category feel able to 'come out' and contribute to discussion and how could they be supported to do so?
- do people and groups to whom the term is attached see themselves as 'socially excluded'? For example, there are many ways in which mental health service users are excluded, for instance, from employment opportunities, through restrictions on their rights, by being unable to adopt a child, access NHS fertility treatment, obtain life insurance, secure entry visas and work permits (for example, McNamara, 1996: 199; Steinberg, 1997: 86–88). Do people conceive of these in terms of exclusion, or perhaps oppression and discrimination?
- is it helpful to understand people's identities in terms of either being socially included or excluded? Can the same person not be both at the same or at different times or in different roles and relationships?
- is social exclusion likely to have shared meanings for the different groups associated with it. What are the implications for discussion if they do not?
- the term is used to include overlapping groups of people who are poor, use social care services and are processed by the criminal justice system. Do members of one group identify and have common concerns with others; for example, poor women, young or older people in care, with sexual abusers and violent criminals? If not, what are the implications for inclusive debate?
- is social exclusion an inherently negative idea if it is not clearly connected with economic exclusion?

Taking debate forward

We have framed these issues as a series of questions because there are as yet no clear answers to most of them. They highlight the problematic nature of inclusive debate about social exclusion and the need to avoid approaching it with uncritical enthusiasm. At the same time, there is reason for some confidence and optimism. There is increasing evidence that groups identified as socially excluded want to contribute to discussions about them and policies affecting them. This is reflected in a growing number of initiatives (ATD Fourth World, 1996; Beresford and Turner, 1997; UK Coalition Against Poverty, Participation Sub-Group, 1997; Beresford et al., 1998). We also know that where movements have engaged in dominant discussions, they have been able to challenge traditional categories, meanings and terms of debate.

However, there are obstacles to a fully inclusive debate which remain insuperable, notably the impossibility of including people who have been totally excluded through sterilisation, screening and abortion programmes which target groups associated with social exclusion; those who have restricted access to medical treatment; and those who have their lives deliberately cut short as, for example, Robert Perske discusses in the USA with regard to people with learning disabilities on death row (Perske, 1991; Wolfensberger, 1992 and 1994; Channel

4 News, 1997; Freedland, 1997).

Some subjects of social policy and social work may resist involvement in debate because its terms are unacceptable. They may not wish to participate, for example, if:

- they have experienced systematic abuse and oppression by the service system (see Wardhaugh and Wilding, 1993) and fear (re)victimisation if they voice views and ideas about their experiences;
- they are viewed as unable to make valid or valuable contributions or have their analyses dismissed or ridiculed because of their supposed 'lack of objectivity' (Lindow, 1994) or 'intellectual deficiency';
- the debate centres upon and perpetuates negative and offensive views of its subjects.

Other obstacles in the way of inclusive debate which must be addressed relate more to the failure of traditional discussions to ensure full and equal access to the subjects of social policy. These relate to:

- the support needs of people with physical, intellectual and sensory impairments, people who communicate differently and people experiencing distress;
- the categorisation of individuals and groups included in the category of social exclusion in terms of 'deserving' and 'undeserving' and conventional reluctance to include the latter;
- the dismissal of subjects of social policy and their organisations as 'unrepresentative', particularly when their views conflict with the status quo (Beresford and Campbell, 1994).

While we have concerns about the inherent problems and practical possibility of an inclusive debate about social exclusion, it is only by attempting such debate that these can be addressed and any progress made on them. Without the involvement of those identified as socially excluded, existing powerholders and discussants will retain control over the idea and category of social exclusion and those included within it. While inclusive debate about social exclusion may be difficult, perhaps impossible to achieve and is open to question, unless preliminary efforts are made to include the subjects of such policy and analysis in its discussion and development, then the most negative expressions of the idea are likely to be reinforced and prevail.

To set in train an inclusive debate means working towards equality between subjects and non-subjects in the debate, in three main areas. These areas are:

1. Equality of respect
The same respect should be attached to the subjects of social exclusion as to other participants in the debate, without any imposition of stigma or assumption of their inadequacy or inferiority, challenging rather than reinforcing dominant discriminations.

2. Equality of validity of contributions

Contributions to the debate from people identified as socially excluded must be accorded the same validity as others. Assumptions about objective, neutral and value free social science cannot be sustained. Recognition should be given to the validity of the subjective knowledges, analyses and perspectives of people included in the category.

3. Equality of ownership and control of the debate and of knowledge

More than a few token users must be included in debate and they should have equal ownership of it. There needs to be a shift in power, in the control of knowledge and what counts as knowledge, with those identified as socially excluded having more say in both.

This is not happening yet. Key requirements for working for inclusive debate include:

* *support for people to take part in discussion about social exclusion.* This includes information, practical support, support for people to increase their confidence and self-esteem, development costs, personal assistance, etc. (Croft and Beresford, 1993b);
* *support for equal opportunities* to ensure that everyone can take part on equal terms regardless of age, 'race', gender, sexuality, disability, distress, or class;
* *opportunities for their own debate* for people included in the category who wish to, to get together, explore and develop their own ideas, agendas and discussion on their own, in safety and confidence, prior to, as well as in addition to taking part in;
* *open debate which includes them on equal terms.*

Supporting inclusive debate

We see support for more inclusive debate about social exclusion as part of a broader commitment which both social work and social policy disciplines need to make to inclusive discussion in their own analysis and development. Social work and social policy commentators and analysts have an important part to play in encouraging inclusive debate about social exclusion. Many, if not most social work service users are associated with social exclusion. Because of this, the policy and theory of social exclusion are likely to play a defining role in the future role and nature of social work, determining whether its future emphasis will be on social control or support; on regulating or including people. This makes it especially important that social work pursues its own inclusive discussion of social exclusion alongside and feeding into other broader debates on the subject. If social work is to be true to its stated professional ethic of self-determination and empowerment, then this must begin with the nature of its discussions about itself and service users. These must be participatory. Because of its potential impact upon them, any social policy research paradigm or agenda should be developed in close association with those included in the category of social exclusion.

CHAPTER 9

Ethnic Minorities and the Criminal Justice System: Exclusion by Choice or Design?

Navnit Dholakia

Introduction

In April 1968, the late Enoch Powell MP gave his famous 'Rivers of Blood' speech to the West Midlands Area Conservative Political Centre in Birmingham. He articulated the threat that black and Asian immigrants posed to the national identity. A lot of changes have taken place since. Britain is now a multi-racial, multi-cultured society and ethnic minorities make a valuable contribution to the everyday lives of people in Britain.

One area of contention, however, both among minority ethnic groups and commentators alike is their over-representation in the criminal justice system: over-representation at least as suspects, defendants and offenders. This contrasts sharply with their under-representation among those administering criminal justice – senior police officers, prosecutors, lawyers, judges, magistrates and prison governors.

This chapter examines the marginalisation of black people and the process by which discriminatory practices, perceived or otherwise, could be redressed if not eliminated. The chapter starts by presenting the current situation within its historical context of immigration and settlement in this country. It then moves on to the nature of discrimination generally and how such discrimination operates in the context of the criminal justice system. Section 95 of the Criminal Justice Act (1991) is explored in relation to its impact on ethnic monitoring and the criminal justice system. It is suggested that there is a pressing need to restore the confidence of minority communities in the administration of justice and some practical measures to tackle discrimination are outlined. Finally, this chapter concludes with a new vision for the future which reflects the diversity of our society as we move into the next century.

An historical perspective

The principle of equality before the law is rightly cherished; it had to be fought for, and in many parts of the world it still has to be won. But we ought not to get carried away with this. Social exclusion can be by choice or by design. Legal exclusion is rather different. There is no choice. But any such provision would smack of apartheid. No civilised society would tolerate such actions. However, I do want to demonstrate that despite legal provision to outlaw discrimination, such as the 1976 Race Relations Act, differential treatment is still the outcome of many decisions we take in this country in relation to minority ethnic groups within the criminal justice system.

I have been involved in 'race' relations for over 30 years. For as long as I can remember I have expressed my concern about the rights of minority groups: the right to live in peace, to get an education, to get a job, to raise a family free from fear and, above all, the right to be treated fairly without reference to 'race', colour, national or ethnic origin. These issues are at the core of the controversy surrounding ethnicity, 'race' and social exclusion. They stand at the heart of every debate on the matter. No longer can a society remain harmonious and at peace, really live with itself and really prosper, if in that society an individual or an establishment denies the right to these ideals by directly or indirectly discriminating against others.

Many statutory agencies are unwilling to give credence to any suggestion that social systems might treat people from different ethnic backgrounds in an unequal manner. The slogan often branded about is that justice, after all, is colour blind and impartial. Try telling this to black and Asian people in this country. Trends in race relations show that racial discrimination is still persisting at a depressingly high level. Minorities are still to be found disproportionately among the poor, the unemployed, the homeless, those who have never worked, those who are stopped and searched, in penal and mental institutions, among the under-achievers in schools and among victims of racial harassment and violence. It has been suggested that the black population is fast becoming an 'underclass' within the UK, insofar as, if employed at all, they tend to have the least desirable, least secure and poorest paid jobs. However, the term 'underclass' is not a euphemism for black discrimination in the UK, as it is in the USA, where the term originated. Blacks in Britain account for only 5 per cent of the total population, and whilst they are over-represented amongst the most socially excluded groups, they do not dominate any of these groups (Roberts, 1997).

Racism and racial discrimination are everyday realities in the lives of minority ethnic groups. Geographically and economically they are in the precarious position of being in the same lowly position which was allocated to them or their forebears when they first came to Britain. But the most frightening aspect is the failure of many of our institutions to take into account the cultural diversity of our different communities.

Primary immigration to this country is rigidly controlled and is virtually at a standstill, with the exception of the rights of wives (often with children) to join their husbands who are lawfully settled here. We are no longer talking of newcomers. More than half of the ethnic minority population was born here. The optimistic assumptions that were made by policy makers when we first migrated to this land have not been realised: that Britain was a true melting pot; that the many racial, cultural and religious groups would all be assimilated into a new whole; and that there would be a single people with similar ideals, attitudes and values. The process was thought to be automatic and inevitable.

But how wrong they were. The process was not automatic or inevitable. Among those of European ancestry there had indeed been considerable assimilation to the political, economical and religious life of the community. This continues even now. Ethnic minority groups, however, have to a great extent retained their identities. Never before has Britain seen such a pluralistic society supplemented by the visual identity of the many individuals within it. The shades of colonial encounters – the master-servant relationship – were no longer the realities of the colonies: they had come to Britain to roost. We then knew that it was a long hard road ahead and we were right.

The nature and extent of discrimination

We must accept that, however much the legal system treats individuals and institutions as equals, it cannot by itself alter the profound inequalities in practice; law is at best a limited instrument with which to seek a greater social justice. Judges, tribunals and magistrates tend to treat equality before the law as a formal concept concerning equal access to the courts and tribunals and also to legal procedures and remedies, but not as a principle which entitles them, within the narrow compass of the legal system, to restrain a stronger party from oppressing a weaker one. We have 'race' relations legislation in Britain. It is an unequivocal declaration of public policy and gives support to those who do not wish to discriminate. It gives protection and redress to minorities and provides for orderly resolution of grievances.

My starting point is that despite a long history of settlement of black and Asian communities in Britain, 'race' relations remain fragile and many of the issues affecting them are discussed on fairly emotive grounds. We live, rhetorically at least, in a fair and just society and all reasonable people would condemn racism and racial discrimination. But we find it difficult to accept that many of the practices we adopt may lead to discriminatory outcomes. Often decisions which are discriminatory are justified on the basis of statutory responsibilities. This is nothing short of institutional racism.

I have often been asked how to identify racial discrimination. Let me pose some basic questions. Do minorities get a fair share of services that are being provided? Are they getting the same quality of treatment as white people? Do they show the same level of satisfaction? Are there significant differences and if so what are the reasons for them? The most important question policy makers need to address is: can they justify the decision on a non-racial basis? If the answer is 'no' then I have no doubt that discrimination may be occurring. Policy makers often profess to be totally committed to racial justice but there is no way in which minorities, who have met enough discrimination and who have had enough bad experiences could have faith in such a platitude.

It is safe to assume that discrimination occurs in all fields. Much research has confirmed that this is so. If you accept that, then if the selection process is right and the broad cross-section of the society is involved, some local authorities, some employers, some residents, some planners and dare I say some judges will hold prejudiced views.

Persons working in the criminal justice agencies represent the same strengths and weaknesses as society as a whole and as the communities from which they come. Research undertaken recently (IPPR, 1997) gives some interesting facts about attitudes towards ethnic minority groups. Only 6 per cent of the white population say that they are not at all prejudiced. Ninety per cent of whites think that people are prejudiced and that the main targets of such prejudice are

Pakistanis (cited by 44 per cent) Indians (37 per cent) Caribbeans (36 per cent) and Africans (31 per cent). It can be assumed, also, that these attitudes are reflected amongst practitioners and policy makers within the criminal justice system.

The IPPR study identified four distinct categories of people:

1. The die hards ('I hate them, I admit it');
2. The I am not racist buts... ('I don't care what colour someone's skin is, but they can't come over here and get more than we do');
3. The comfortable liberals ('having a good education has enabled me to see how stupid racism is'); and
4. The young optimist ('racists are stupid, how can you judge everyone just by the colour they are').

Coupled with these attitudes held by the general public are the more covert perceptions and practices of the institutions of the state, where it is increasingly argued that evidence of institutionalised racism is overwhelming (Scraton and Chadwick, 1996). The police service in Britain is a case in point. As Hall (1996) suggests:

> Not all the stories and rumours [of police prejudice] are, of course, true. Not all of them are traceable to racism within the local police forces. But when all the reasonable allowances have been made, this series of episodes leaves us with no other conclusion than that the police have undertaken, whether willingly or no, to constrain by means which would not long stand up to inspection within the rule of law, an alienated black population and thereby, to police the social crisis of our cities (1996: 266).

The Home Office has tried to suggest that it is an individual, attitudinal problem rather than an institutional one – the statistics and the experience of black people themselves open this claim up to intense criticism, to the point that many commentators now feel that racism is being reproduced on a scale that cannot be explained away by 'scapegoating' or mere prejudice (Keith, 1996). Sim et al. (1987) also point to the role of institutionalised racism in exacerbating the further marginalisation and social exclusion of minority ethnic groups:

> Marginalization is not a 'condition' suddenly inflicted on the Afro-Caribbean or Asian community simply by a downturn in the economy. It is written into the statutory definitions of immigration law and reflected in the political management of identities throughout state practices (Sim et al., 1987, quoted in Scraton and Chadwick, 1996: 291).

Racial discrimination and criminal justice

At a NACRO conference in 1995, the then most senior criminal law judge, the late Lord Chief Justice, Lord Taylor, said that race issues go to the heart of our system of justice, which demands that all are treated as equals before the law (Taylor, 1995). It is, therefore, a matter of the gravest concern if members of the ethnic minorities feel they are discriminated against by the criminal justice system: more so if their fears are borne out by experience. Of course, Lord Taylor's statement reflects a commitment at the highest level of criminal justice agencies to ensure that the system of justice is free from any kind of racial discrimination, and that it can be seen to be so. Nevertheless, fears have been expressed – and experience suggests – that racial discrimination persists within the criminal justice system, especially in relation to young black people, a matter which is of serious concern to us all.

When someone enters the criminal justice system, first, through coming to the attention of the police, a series of decisions is made by a succession of different agencies – the police, the crown prosecution service, social workers or probation officers, the courts and finally the prisons. At various stages in the criminal justice process there is scope for discretion in making decisions. If discrimination – whether intended or not – occurs at any of these stages, it will have a cumulative effect on what happens next, all the way through the system, being reflected eventually in the prison population figures. It is essential, therefore, that the process of decision making within the criminal justice system is free from any form of discrimination, direct or indirect, and that it can be shown to be so. This has not always been the case. There is now widespread concern, which is reinforced by research evidence, that the system treats black offenders more harshly than white offenders. Blacks are also disproportionately represented as 'clients' within the system compared with their counterparts on the staff. Denney (1992) suggests that only 1.9 per cent of all probation officers in England and Wales are black and that there are few black representatives in other sectors of the criminal justice system; for example, among judges, lawyers and magistrates.

Certainly the disproportionate numbers of black people, and particularly young black people in prisons, suggests that discrimination is evident. The latest available Home Office figures show that 16 per cent of the male prison population and 26 per cent of the female prison population are from minority ethnic groups, when such groups comprise just over 5 per cent of the general population (Home Office, 1997). Analysis of the prison population over the past few years has shown that black and Asian males are serving longer sentences than whites; there are significant differences in sentence lengths for males between ethnic groups even after allowing for factors such as offence type, the type of court at which the sentence was passed, and the number of previous convictions (Home Office, 1994).

A PSI survey among 16 and 17 year-olds found that only 1 in 12 young black people felt that judges and courts gave everyone fair and equal treatment (Shaw, 1994). This finding is augmented by evidence amassed in the past two decades which seems to demonstrate stark differences in dealing with black as opposed to white suspects and defendants. For example, according to a report of the Royal Commission of Criminal Justice (FitzGerald, 1993):

- black youths are especially likely to be stopped by the police, although only a small proportion (approximately 10 per cent) of these stops result in arrests being made;
- once arrested black youngsters are less likely to be cautioned than whites;
- the overall pattern of charges brought against blacks differs from that of whites;
- black defendants are more likely to be remanded in custody;
- black defendants are more likely to plead not guilty to the charges against them;
- black defendants are more likely to be tried at Crown Courts;
- black defendants are more likely to be acquitted;
- black defendants found guilty of crime are likely to receive more and longer custodial sentences and a different range of non-custodial disposals.

The workings of the system generally are characterised by considerable variations. The impact of these variations falls unevenly on black groups. The decisions of the criminal justice agencies tend to interact with and compound each other. None of these can be viewed in isolation; for if there are even small differences in key decisions taken by each, the cumulative impact is very large indeed.

Ethnic monitoring

Section 95 of the 1991 Criminal Justice Act provides a constructive opportunity to promote non-discriminatory practice. This important legislation was the first time that an obligation on criminal justice agencies to avoid discrimination was set out in statute (the Race Relations Act (1976) did not cover the criminal justice system). The 1991 Act requires the Secretary of State in each year to publish information as considered expedient for the purpose of:

- enabling persons engaged in the administration of justice to become aware of the financial implications of their decisions;
- facilitating the performance of such persons of their duty to avoid discriminating against any person on the ground of race or sex or any other improper ground.

The latter clause has been widely interpreted to mean the setting up and use of systems of ethnic monitoring. To date, four reports on 'race' have been published (in 1992, 1994, 1995 and 1997), including one on 'race' and gender. The most recent report on 'race' was published in December 1997 and includes information and analysis on the first full year of police monitoring of stop and searches; arrests; cautions; homicides; victims of crime; the prison population and the composition of the work forces in all the criminal justice agencies (Home Office, 1997).

However, caution must be exercised since Section 95 does not require the publication of information for its own sake. The purpose is to assist practitioners to avoid discrimination. The tragedy is that the only reliable data we have currently are the statistics but these are the end products of a system in which discrimination may have been cumulatively occurring.

We are still not clear about the purpose of monitoring and collection of information. We need to ask what information is needed and what works, what are the pitfalls, and what are the practical difficulties. We need to collect statistical information and research findings which will establish whether black people are treated equitably by the criminal justice system. If they are not, then we need to establish reasons and indicate ways of rectifying the situation.

Within criminal justice agencies, however, there is still a half-hearted approach made to monitoring key decisions in the system. For example:

Plea
It would be helpful to know how much influence legal advisers have in entering a plea on behalf of their clients. Does a 'not guilty' plea increase the tariff on sentencing if guilt is proved?

Whether offender was charged or cautioned
A study by the Commission for Racial Equality in a number of police areas confirmed that black youngsters were less likely to be cautioned and more likely to be charged than their white counterparts (Commission for Racial Equality, 1992).

Types of offence with which black people are charged and the level of seriousness
Monitoring would identify the types of offences with which black people are charged more frequently. It would also help to identify the seriousness of such offences and whether bail or remand before trial had a bearing on the ultimate sentence passed. It is obvious that when black people are charged with 'either way' offences in Magistrates' Courts, they prefer to appear before a jury in the Crown Courts. We ought to establish reasons for this.

There are a number of ways in which we can address a problem. Take mugging for example. We can address the offending behaviour of our youngsters or alternatively we can lock up all the old ladies. It is however unacceptable to target the whole black community with operations like Eagle Eye[1] for the sake of a small number of black and white offenders.

Maintaining confidence and challenging discrimination
Discrimination exists in all walks of life. The criminal justice system is no exception. We must be able to identify discrimination and take measures to eliminate it. If not, the criminal justice system will command little confidence in the black community.

---

1. Operation Eagle Eye' was launched in July, 1995 by the Metropolitan Police. This was aimed at young, black people involved in street robberies.

I started by saying that equality had no meaning unless it was accompanied by fairness, respect and dignity. Let me conclude with the example of a young black whose letter to a Chief Constable was forwarded to me at the Police Complaints Authority. I quote this letter in full:

> On Monday 20 December I had occasion to deliver an item to someone living in Harlow. After taking the U-turn off from the M11 I realised that I did not have the faintest idea where the place was, and that upon stopping to look for the directions I had been given, discovered that I had left them at home. I had by now pulled over off the roundabout; as I looked into my rear view window a police car was just pulling up behind me. I quickly got out of my vehicle and showed the two officers the address that I had written down. They explained where I should go but as the area was completely alien to me I was having trouble taking in the information. They said 'follow me' and within minutes I was at my destination.
>
> I could not get over the fact that they went to all this trouble for me and were so polite and courteous, the reason is that a) I am twenty years old; b) I am black; and c) I drive a C reg. 950cc Fiesta which I take a pride in keeping clean. These are three factors that for some reason have always made police officers in the past change from beauty to the beast and while I do not have so much as a driving offence, it has always been assumed by any police officer that I have spoken to, for whatever reason, that I must have a criminal record and therefore must be giving wrong information regarding my name etc.
>
> Therefore you can imagine my surprise when these two officers of yours were not only very helpful, but that they also treated me as a human being. I must say it was very refreshing. I would like you to thank them on my behalf and let them know that they have gone a long way in restoring my faith in the police force. I would like to say that I have always respected law and order even though it has never respected me. On Monday I felt respected.

It is not so much what the law or declaration specifically says but rather the general underlying attitudes and values which it is held to express that are of importance for social well-being. Equality should never be undermined. In the final analysis the emphasis in any policy determination should be the manner in which and the extent to which minorities' deepest feelings about their race, colour, national or ethnic origin are truly accepted within the community and by the policy makers. The difficulties faced by black and Asian people are merely a symptom of the wider issues confronting them in this country. The law seems to have two faces as far as they are concerned. We not only confront those who are part of the immigration process but the perception of the minorities is that we then turn towards the stranger within. I suspect, therefore, that the unease felt by minorities simply cannot be resolved on legal grounds or by use of the existing legislation. This has been tried and failed. So how do we challenge discrimination?

First, there has to be a commitment at the top of every organisation to recognise discrimination and to adopt and enforce measures to prevent its recurrence. Secondly, there must be a public statement to that effect. It is not a substitute for action but part of it. It is a recognition that there will be racial discrimination and that we want to tackle it. If such a statement can be publicised in places where it is accessible to minorities then the barriers and suspicions can begin to be broken down. Thirdly, a mere publication of a statement is not enough. There should be a proper system of monitoring which checks on outcomes. Let me draw an analogy with the health and safety legislation. We are all against accidents. Accidents are not a good thing. But without a proper system, management is ill-equipped to bridge the gap between asserting that something should not happen and ensuring that it does not. Fourthly, equality targets as part of an equal opportunity policy are essential. These are not quotas nor must they be achieved by discriminatory practices. Fifthly, positive action and not positive discrimination must be actively pursued. It means recognising and developing potential which has not been used because of past discrimination and disadvantage. Sixthly, we must set out clear objectives for training and such training must be capable of evaluation. Finally, equal opportunity does not simply mean good employment practices. It must be accompanied by equality in the provision and delivery of services. The bottom line is to ensure that the equal opportunity policy is honest, decent, legal and true.

A vision for the future

What is evident is that there is a conflict between the concept of what is appropriate in eliminating discrimination and what is required. But more fundamentally we should, after 50 years of our settlement here, be asking some pertinent questions. What sort of society do we want to take forward into the next century? We need a vision about the kind of future we want to achieve. The purpose of the vision is to motivate people. We need a new mission statement for the millennium that will identify the distinctive route chosen to achieve goals, but above all we need first to identify goals which are realistic and achievable.

The main ingredients must be to build confidence amongst the minorities in the structures that are in place, to ensure that we participate from within, that we communicate with policymakers and above all that we identify as stakeholders in the process of law and citizenship. What is now required is political wisdom appropriate to our multiracial, multicultural and multi-religious society. Let me conclude by quoting the late Lord Boyle of Handsworth:

> Political wisdom consists in trying to narrow the gap between the value which men and women place on their own personalities, and value placed on them by the community within which they live; furthermore no community can afford for long to deny the application of this principal to racial minorities as well.

The treatment received by racial minorities must concern us all, for if we at any time deny them their rights then we are weakening our own claims to such ideals.

Conclusions

I have tried in this chapter to take a longer-term perspective and to outline the positive as well as the negative developments since the late 1960s. There have been several positive developments, not least the creation in 1992 of the Ethnic Minorities Advisory Committee of the Judicial Studies Board, which has developed training in race issues for the judiciary and which is now embarking on equal treatment training for lay magistrates. When the Criminal Justice Consultative Council was created in 1993, it took up race issues as one of the first items on its agenda. The result was a sub-committee report on Race and the Criminal Justice System which set out 50 recommendations for criminal justice agencies and for the 23 Area Criminal Justice Liaison Committees that were also created in the same year (Home Office, 1993).

At senior levels within the criminal justice system, there is without doubt a commitment to make positive changes and to tackle inequalities. But we have still not succeeded in translating this into action at the crucial points – on the street, in the courts and in the prisons. Nor have we yet convinced the minority ethnic communities themselves that these positive changes might bring about a better deal for them or that they themselves should perhaps consider careers in the criminal justice agencies.

The most recent figures for 1996 suggest that while minority ethnic groups make up just over five per cent of the population, they nevertheless represent 20 per cent of the people stopped and searched. Amongst those held on remand in young offender institutions in England and Wales, the black population can be as high as nearly 60 per cent (NACRO, unpublished).

In taking this longer retrospective look, I am far from convinced that we have really even started to get to grips with these disparities. The Crime and Disorder Bill will soon be enacted and will introduce many new measures to deal with young people in trouble with the law. Will young black people get equal access to prevention and employment programmes? Or will they, yet again, be over-represented among the 'heavy-end' offenders, more likely to be curfewed, electronically tagged and imprisoned?

To bring to an end the social exclusion of minority ethnic communities within the criminal justice system – as offenders, victims and employees – should be a paramount aim for all concerned.

CHAPTER 10

Social Work with Offenders: The Practice of Exclusion and the Potential for Inclusion

David Smith

Introduction

This chapter begins in gloom and then attempts to find reasons for optimism. The gloom comes specifically from recent experience in Britain, or more accurately in England and Wales, of government pressure on the probation service to abandon its social work roots and traditions and become something more like a community penalties enforcement agency; and this against the background of a punitive penal policy which has seen an increase of 50 per cent in the prison population in less than five years. In moving from gloom to greater optimism I will try to show that there are potential links to be made between some of social work's traditional values and skills and recent trends and developments in criminology, drawing in the process on feminist ethics, social theory and ecology. In some ways my conclusions are familiar ones, but they are reached by a less than familiar route. For my purposes here, creative social work in this context is work which tends to promote the social inclusion of offenders, or those at risk of offending, rather than stigmatising and outcasting them. First, though, back to the gloom.

One of the paradoxes of the current scene is that recent years have seen a revival of optimism about the possibility that social work with offenders can demonstrate its effectiveness in terms of reducing the risk of re-offending (for example, McGuire, 1995). Instead of the grim consolations of the belief that 'nothing works', we can now say at the very least that some things work better than other things, and that we can more or less specify what these are. This shift (at its best, a shift from naive pessimism to a cautious, rational, empirically informed optimism) is in itself a most welcome development, but we should remember that the evidence on which it is based relates, for quite understandable reasons, to one form of practice only – intensive groupwork with relatively persistent offenders – and that comparatively little is known about other aspects of practice. The literature – much of it Canadian – tells us that 'community-based' programmes are, other things being equal, more likely to be effective than institutionally-based ones, but this has notably failed to have an impact on recent penal policy and sentencing practice, either in Britain or North America: official faith in social work with offenders, and particularly in the probation service, has diminished just as practitioners were starting to believe that they really could make a worthwhile difference. The probation service in England and Wales has been endlessly told that public confidence in its work needs to be restored, that sentencers lack faith in community penalties, and so on – a wonderfully self-fulfilling prophecy. Its work has been redefined as 'punishment in the community', the training of its new recruits has been firmly separated from social work training, and through this process the service has tried to respond dutifully by 'confronting offending behaviour', and demonstrating its commitment to the rigorous enforcement of orders – by showing how tough-minded it can be; but of course it can never be as tough-minded as prison.

What is it that is lost as a result? As Drakeford and Vanstone (1996) have argued, an exclusive stress on offending behaviour entails the expectation that offenders, and not their social circumstances, must change, and encourages the abstraction of the offending act itself from the personal and relational context which could make it intelligible. Social work with offenders is redefined in a language of hostility, aggression and warfare, in which offenders must be tackled, confronted, and challenged – the language of the political rhetoric which has dominated the discourse of penal policy in recent years; and it is a rhetoric which has real effects: 'The deeply offensive image of young criminals as hyenas (featured in a Home Office crime prevention campaign on television) is a self-fulfilling prophecy: given no other role, that is what they will become' (Arnold and Jordan, 1996: 41). Social work with offenders risks becoming implicated in the further exclusion and marginalisation of already marginalised and vulnerable social groups. In addition, with the announcement that electronic tagging is to be extended, it seems clear that policies of segregation, stigmatisation and control are likely to persist. Unless some alternative strategy can be developed, social work agencies are liable to become incorporated into the implementation of such policies. My main theme in this chapter is an outline of the possible elements of such an alternative, which draws on aspects of feminist ethics, theories of late modernity and ecological concerns as well as on research on practice; but first, I want to indicate some ways in which social work already contributes, or can contribute, to the marginalisation and exclusion of offenders.

The practice of exclusion

It probably hardly needs to be said that the population of known offenders contains many people who are excluded from full social participation in ways which their status as offenders compounds and complicates. Every survey of probation caseloads (and of the prison population) tells the same story (for example, Dodd and Hunter, 1992; Stewart and Stewart, 1993). Compared with the general population, known offenders are much more likely to be unemployed, to be poor, to have truanted or been excluded from school (Devlin, 1995), to have left school with no qualifications, to be homeless or insecurely housed, to have experienced a disrupted, unhappy or abusive family life, to have been in the care of local authorities, to have physical and mental health problems, often associated with alcohol or drug misuse, and to have been victims of crime. Their social exclusion predates their offending, and goes well beyond non-participation in the labour market. Criminological theory and research have long suggested that offending rates are higher among oppressed and disadvantaged social groups, and that the further exclusion which they are likely to suffer when they encounter the criminal justice system increases the risk of offending – and especially of persistent and serious offending – by encouraging affiliation to criminal subcultures (Braithwaite, 1989). If one is interested in crime reduction and community safety, there is a strong argument for penal and social policies and practices which are inclusionary and reintegrative – the opposite of those currently in favour with the proponents of the war against crime.

The clearest form of exclusion available is incarceration, and there is evidence that social workers can increase the risk of imprisonment, and not always unwittingly (Raynor et al., 1994). A commitment to 'anti-custodialism' as a social work value (Nellis, 1995) would be fundamental to a social work agency concerned with promoting social inclusion, and would find its practical expression in effective influence on sentencers' decisions. Research suggests, however, that the general effect of social workers' court reports is to change the distribution of non-custodial sentences rather than to reduce the use of custody (Moxon, 1988; Raynor, 1991). Such evidence as there is on what makes for effective court report practice suggests (Gelsthorpe and Raynor, 1995) that better reports are more likely to produce non-custodial sentences, a pre-requisite for any kind of creative practice, so that quality control of court reports and systematic monitoring of the effects of social work intervention in court are essential if practice is to have inclusionary rather than exclusionary effects. Careless or incompetent reports, not to mention stigmatising and rejecting ones, can directly contribute to social exclusion, and there is a basic moral responsibility to be critically aware of social work's impact on the system's operation.

Another way in which social work can foster the segregation and marginalisation of vulnerable people is by running 'community-based' programmes which in reality have no base in the community. One of the limitations of the effectiveness research is that it has generally failed to attend to the question of what supportive networks an intensive programme requires if it is to be effective. There is some evidence that without such networks even coherent and well-delivered programmes which show promising early results will find it difficult to maintain their effectiveness for long (Raynor and Vanstone, 1996). The 'what works' research is also largely silent on the question of what help and support with personal and social difficulties are needed to give intensive programmes a chance of being effective. This is one consequence of the kind of thinking which wrenches the act of offending from its social context and views it solely as a piece of behaviour which the individual offender must be persuaded to avoid in future. So-called 'welfare' problems – exactly those which used to make up the domain of social work's intervention – have been declared to be none of the social worker's business; instead the task is to follow the manual and deliver the programme and maintain its integrity, with appropriately decisive action in the event of unjustifiable absences, and with no nonsense about the quality of the relationship between worker and client – let alone about social work skills and values. The result of this approach, pursued in its full rigour, will be the further exclusion of the already excluded; their status as offenders will become their main, or only, status, and the rights and claims they have on the rest of us by virtue of their common citizenship will be increasingly ignored and ineffectual.

The American penal reformer Jerome Miller (cited in Pepinsky, 1991) has said that there are only two kinds of criminologists, those who think criminals are different from themselves and those who do not. One of the virtues of social work with offenders, as I see it, is that it could draw on social work's resources, such as its stress on self-understanding and empathy, to ensure that its practitioners remained aware of what they and their clients had in common, rather than seeing them as alien, threatening, or less than human; but if social work agencies become electronic tagging agencies, they will firmly have joined the criminologists who see offenders as radically unlike themselves, and become practitioners of exclusion and social division rather than of inclusion and integration.

The potential for inclusion

I want now to begin to suggest some of the elements of a social work strategy which might prove effective in resisting these tendencies. First and most modestly, I want to suggest some implications for social work agencies seriously committed to promoting the social inclusion of offenders. John Stewart and I have argued elsewhere at greater length for this approach (Smith and Stewart, 1997), and I will not rehearse the arguments here, except to say that they are based on a concern to make 'community-based' mean something more than 'not actually in prison'. Some principles which a social work agency interested in strengthening the community basis of its work might follow are set out in Figure 1.

Figure 1: Some organisational elements of community-based practice

- Decentralisation: offices as community resources, located in the areas they are meant to serve.
- Accessibility: rather than fortresses, offices should be open and welcoming, offering a range of services and resources (advice, information, child care, facilities for fun and adventure).
- Diversification: employment of a wider range of people with a wider range of skills, including youth workers, community workers, trainers, 'social pedagogues'.
- Networking: building on existing skills and knowledge to develop supportive links with the resources on which intensive work depends for its success.
- Developing and disseminating knowledge: little is known by anyone, and nothing is known by many, about crucial aspects of practice (for example in community safety, partnerships, restorative justice).

(adapted from Smith and Stewart, 1997)

The first three items on this list are, in principle, capable of being achieved by a single agency acting on its own initiative and within its own resources. They are all about encouraging less defensive, suspicious practice, and about moving away from punishment and regulation towards a more generous and optimistic view of what social work with offenders might entail. They aim to address issues beyond offending behaviour, to promote the non-stigmatic elements of social work with offenders, and to reduce the likelihood that offenders themselves will regard contact with the agency as an inherently negative, punitive experience. There is recent evidence (Rex, 1997) that, as in the past, many people on probation like their probation officers and appreciate their efforts to help, and, importantly, that the perceived quality of the relationship with the officer matters to clients and can influence their behaviour; but the further the service retreats, or is beaten back, into enforcement, regulation and relational distance at the expense of help, support and empathy, the less likely such findings will become. Of course, no social work agency can address all the needs and problems of offenders on its own, so the networking skills which are – or should be – already available will be important, in partnerships both with formal agencies and with, for example, potential employers who (despite the messages of the warmongers) still see helping with the reintegration of offenders as part of their civic duty (Stern, 1996). Finally, because of the narrow focus of so much of the effectiveness research, little is known about what works, what counts as best practice, in many existing areas of work, let alone in the new areas, which a more inclusionary approach to social work with offenders would emphasise, and a critical awareness of the outcomes of one's interventions should be part of the basic moral equipment of the social worker.

Figure 2 is an attempt to suggest some elements of the kind of supportive inter-agency network a specialist project for offenders may need if it is to retain meaningful connections with everyday community life. It is drawn from research, with colleagues, on the Freagarrach project for persistent juvenile offenders, which has sites in Falkirk and Alloa in central Scotland. Freagarrach was conceived from the beginning not as a 'stand alone' project but as one part of a much broader strategy for young people at risk in the region. In our early work on the evaluation of the project people constantly stressed to us that the intensive project was only 'the tip of the iceberg', and could not be understood without knowing what lay beneath the surface, and as our work has progressed we have been increasingly convinced that they were right.

If social workers and probation officers in England and Wales paid more attention to what is happening in other parts of Britain, they might acquire a new and more optimistic sense of what is possible. Here the project's own work, which has in full measure the qualities associated with success in the effectiveness literature, is supported and facilitated in a number of immediately practical ways by the commitment of other agencies. For example, the access to the police database allows the project leader to identify young people who by virtue of the persistence of their offending should be referred to the project, and proactively to pursue referrals rather than relying exclusively on social workers to think of making them. The support from the Education Department has enabled young people who have long been out of school to be gently but successfully reintroduced to the education system, within the context of a broad policy designed to reduce the use of school exclusions and allow prompt intervention in school-based problem behaviour. The Reporters (the officials who act as gate-keepers to the Scottish juvenile justice and child welfare system (the Children's Hearing System)) are kept fully informed of the project's work and adapt their decisions in recognition of the young people's needs for continuity and the benefits that the project brings; and neither they nor anyone else seem to have argued that attendance should be anything other than voluntary. Some such network of inter-agency support and commitment seems likely to be important if the effects of intensive project work are to prove sustainable; without it, the project will tend to stigmatise and exclude despite all the good intentions of its sponsors and staff.

Figure 2: Inter-agency support for an intensive project

Police
• maximum discretion to respond informally
• encouraging young people into sports/leisure facilities
• making database on offending available to project
Education
• provision of day unit places
• anti-exclusion strategy
• secondment of teachers to Reporter's office
• joint work on reintegration
Reporters
• support for voluntary attendance
• willingness to divert from Hearings
Social work
• secondment of staff
• managing conflict in residential homes without calling the police
• keeping faith with the project
Other networks
• peer education on drugs
• alcohol project
• links with colleges and employers

I have so far tended to refer to 'community' as if it were an unproblematic and common-sense concept, when, as everyone knows, it is not. Since I am about to argue that Braithwaite's (1989) theory of reintegrative shaming, and the practices in restorative and relational justice which are increasingly informed by it, represent the most promising line of development for social work and related practice in the field of offending, and since Braithwaite has been criticised for over-reliance on communitarian concepts, I should offer some clarification at this point. Braithwaite (1995) is clear about the differences between the kinds of community that are important for his theory and the position of some influential American communitarians 'for whom it seems to mean beating up your neighbours if you catch them smoking on the street'

(Eagleton, 1997). Braithwaite's uses of the concept of community are summarised in Figure 3.

Figure 3: Braithwaite's communitarianism

Communitarianism I
New social movements/communities of interest (women's movement; environmental movements; campaign against drink-driving)
Communitarianism II
Community accountability conferences (Family Group Conferences) for reintegrative shaming:
• relevant communities mobilised to promote offenders' moral education and moralise about crime
• ceremonies both to certify and decertify deviance
• conveying disapproval while retaining a relationship of respect
• disapproval of the deed without labelling persons as evil
• deviance not allowed to become a master status trait (junkie, bully, etc.)
(adapted from Braithwaite, 1995)

Like Giddens (1994), Braithwaite (1995: 200) is suspicious of any 'utopian yearning for lost geographical community that is not to be found in the contemporary metropolis'. Braithwaite sees this as impractical; Giddens sees it as also potentially dangerous, since such communities exclude as well as include (indeed, are defined by exclusion), and can promote the 'fundamentalism' and cultural segmentation which Giddens associates with violence. Braithwaite's communitarianism is, then, one which recognises the realities of modernity; and he can show that empirically both his versions have produced socially desirable results, in using shame, or the threat of it, to reduce the acceptability in Australia of drink-driving, male violence against women in the home, and industrial pollution, and in the successes of the growing movement of restorative justice, originating in victim-offender mediation and now expanded into family group conferencing and the like (see, for example, Umbreit and Roberts, 1996).

Figure 3 sets out the main elements of conferencing informed by the theory of reintegrative shaming as a response to an offence. The micro-community of the family group or community accountability conference is mobilised to form a network of care and support for both victim and offender; the aim is to reach a resolution of the conflict represented by the offence which will allow both parties to re-assume their everyday social identities, instead of retaining the statuses of victim and offender (both carrying the stigma of difference (see Rock, 1990)). Offenders and their supporters give commitments designed to promote their future good conduct, and offer victims some token, material or symbolic, of reparation and repentance. The element in this which many people find most problematic is that of shame, and it is true that some communitarians have interpreted shame in exclusionary and stigmatising ways, and Braithwaite's own more recent work has tended to play down the need for active shaming of the offender in these situations. It seems clear from research (for example, Smith et al., 1988) that attempts to induce shame by bullying or hectoring denunciation are not only likely to be counter-productive but are irrelevant: shame, for the great majority of offenders, is inherent in the encounter with the victim, and requires no special effort on the part of the mediator or facilitator. We can leave condemnation of the person to the judges. The skills the mediator needs are different – and very much like the skills of social work.

The theory of reintegrative shaming, I have suggested, provides a suitable basis for the practice of restorative justice. Figure 4 summarises the main features of this approach to justice, contrasts them with the comparable features of formal criminal justice systems, and, I hope, connects the values and methods of restorative justice with those of social work.

Figure 4: Characteristics of restorative justice

- reintegration and reacceptance (instead of condemnation, stigmatisation, outcasting)
- promotion of moral education within a network of care (instead of calculating just deserts)
- stress on importance of relationships, empathy, problem-solving (instead of abstract, impersonal, universal rules)
- ethic of care (instead of, or complementary to, ethic of justice)
- peacemaking (instead of warmaking)
- stress on importance of insight and self-understanding
- expression of values associated with social work (respect and care for persons, belief in their capacity to grow and change)

(from Bottoms and Stelman, 1988; Braithwaite, 1989; Masters and Smith, 1998)

In Figure 4 I have deliberately over-drawn the contrasts between the two approaches, since all but the strictest just deserts systems allow for some consideration of the circumstances of individual cases (though there are systems in the United States which do not, and we in Europe have been warned by Christie (1993) that what happens in America will also happen to us). But restorative justice aims to achieve social benefits which are not within the scope of traditional systems of criminal justice (Burnside and Baker, 1994). It is inherently forward-looking or consequentialist rather than backward-looking and retributive. It stresses the importance of relationships and of understanding the offence in the context of offenders' relations with their victims, their families, and their wider social networks. As such it has close affinities, recognised some time ago by Heidensohn (1986), with the 'ethic of care' which Gilligan (1982) suggests is characteristic of feminine approaches to moral dilemmas, in contrast with the 'ethic of justice' which developmental psychology had seen as the highest stage of moral reasoning. I am not suggesting that the disposal of all cases can be informed exclusively by the ethic of care, since the ethic of justice will be needed as a safeguard against arbitrariness, abuse and corruption (Masters and Smith, 1998); but a larger place for the ethic of care in our response to offenders is an essential element of a more inclusionary strategy.

Family group conferencing and similar forms of restorative justice aim to restore a safe social fabric in which dialogue and communication replace coercion and violence. They thus have affinities with the 'peacemaking' movement within critical criminology (Pepinsky and Quinney, 1991; Pepinsky, 1995) and with Giddens's (1994: 124) advocacy of 'dialogic democracy' as the answer to fundamentalism (conceived as 'exactly a refusal of dialogue'). Pepinsky (1995) writes in his 'Peacemaking Primer' on the World Wide Web:

> People cannot talk and listen together and fight one another at the same time. Peacemaking is a matter of injecting quanta of conversation into our social space – conversation which embraces the greatest victims and most powerful oppressors of the moment. The sooner the conversation begins, the less explosive violent reactions have a chance to grow to be, the sooner power imbalances will be mediated, the sooner peace will be made.

The contrast is with warmaking: 'social security lies in the strength of the empathic social fabrics we weave'; or:

> Peacemaking is the art and science of weaving and reweaving oneself with others into a social fabric of mutual love, respect and concern...The other attitude is that of...warmaking. We are all familiar with the art and science of warmaking. We all well know what deterrence is, for example (Pepinsky, 1995).

The importance of insight into oneself and empathy with others has also been stressed in some recent criminological writing not directly associated with the peacemaking movement. Christie (1997) has recently complained that too much criminology is tedious, repetitive and trivial, and suggested that one of the reasons is that the over-socialisation of social scientists leads to a loss of access to oneself: '...in the process of giving room to the authorized perceptions, a depreciation of the importance of one's own personal experiences will take place'. This is especially odd in criminology, since:

> We have sinned and been sinned against, we have acted as law-breakers, as police, as prosecutors, as defenders, as judges, as prison guards....We have also all used alcohol, abused it, or not used it at all and by that very reason had our struggles. We eat and overeat, or maybe just the opposite, and strive to control ourselves or others or to protect ourselves or others from still other people's attempt to control us. We are all continuously torn between lust and loyalties, confronted with dilemmas, often ending up with regrets for our failures. There is so little in the field of criminology we have not yet experienced.

The problem is access to ourselves. Access, and respect for what we find (Christie, 1997: 14–15).

I am making these connections in order to suggest that the reformulation of social work's traditional concerns (about which there has lately been some collective embarrassment in Britain) as a list of largely behavioural 'competencies', which has replaced talk of empathy and the quality of relationships, need not mean that social work is intellectually isolated or exposed. It would be a sad irony if social work were to reject these old values and interests just as criminology and social theory are discovering them. The personalist values of social work listed in Figure 4 (from Bottoms and Stelman, 1988) seem to me essential for effective social work practice, however remote they are from modern managerialism; and they are equally essential for the practice of restorative justice.

Finally, I want to suggest what implications these ideas might have for social work activity in the service of broader crime prevention, or community safety (which Nellis (1995) argues should be one of the core values of probation practice, along with anti-custodialism and restorative justice). In summary, these are as follows: instead of violence, coercion and exclusion, an integrative approach to crime prevention would be concerned with:

- repairing damaged solidarities
- encouraging dialogue and democracy in conflict resolution
- stressing connectedness (to self, others, material and social environment, the ecological milieu)
- advocating social work values of social justice, social cohesion, community safety

The discourse of crime prevention risks being overwhelmed by a language of warmaking and aggression, in which 'zero tolerance' is wrenched from its original context of domestic violence and is used to justify exclusionary practices which strike many thoughtful police officers as dangerous and alienating, and marginalised social groups are criminalised (as in the 1994 Criminal Justice and Public Order Act) and segregated well away from the orderly communities of the law-abiding. A social work presence in community safety efforts is vital if these stigmatising and coercive trends are to be resisted. Among the damaged solidarities (Giddens, 1994)) which social work might help to repair are those of family life, not with any aim of reviving a lost 'traditional' and patriarchal family – another variety of fundamentalism – but by providing practical support and advice to parents and carers under pressure. Braithwaite (1989) is clear that reintegrative shaming is a characteristic of effective parenting and therefore of conscience-building, so that its main value is in preventing 'primary deviance': the child may be sent to his or her room for misbehaviour, but reintegration of the child is signalled by the loving hug which terminates the shaming. Support for families is a key feature of the Scottish project I described earlier, and there is evidence of its effectiveness in reducing the risk of offending (Farrington, 1996).

Another arena whose importance for socialisation Braithwaite stresses is the school. One of the pieces of research which contradicted the 'nothing works' orthodoxy was on the impact of school-based counselling and social work on delinquency rates (Rose and Marshall, 1974), and it is a pity that its implications for practice were never taken up. Some recent work in Belgium (Deklerck and Depuydt, 1995; Depuydt and Deklerck, 1997) suggests what might be done at the level of the school environment rather than with individual children. They counterpoise 'linkedness' (or 'connectedness') to the disintegration of social solidarity which they see as a consequence of modernity. Delinquency is conceived as a loss of connectedness, and their work in schools, whose early results are promising, aims to make children more aware of the ways in which they are linked to their own inner selves, to others, to their material and social environment, and to what Depuydt and Deklerck call 'the ecological milieu'. At each level children are encouraged to consider the importance of these links, and the need to maintain them through responsible and considerate behaviour. Quiet periods for rest and reflection have been built into the school timetable, to promote insight and self-understanding; new methods of conflict resolution have been tried, including peer mediation to resolve disputes; children are encouraged to think about the origins of the materials they use, and to care for their immediate physical environment; the link with society is fostered through opportunities for participation in writing the school's regulations, periods of collective celebration, and the involvement of parents in school life; and a sense of connection with the global environment is developed by allowing the children to plant small vegetable gardens, to enable them to 'make contact with the circle of nature' (Depuydt and Deklerck, 1997). All these initiatives, though developed independently, have close parallels in the reintegrative and relational disciplinary practices in Japanese schools (Masters, 1997a; 1997b) – which appear to make an important contribution to Japan's status as the only large industrial society whose crime rate has declined (rather than spectacularly increased) over the past 50 years.

Although some of the materials I have used here may be unfamiliar in the context of social work, the arguments themselves produce what turns out to be a fairly traditional, though I hope not fundamentalist, set of values for social work and ideas for its practice. If, with Bottoms (1989) and Nellis (1995), one extends the standard account of social work's values to include such less individualistic concepts of social cohesion, social justice, and community safety, it is possible to suggest that the trends identified here in social theory, criminology and criminal justice practice (influences from feminist psychology and philosophy and from ecology, underpinned by the theory of reintegrative shaming), provide opportunities and openings for creative social work practice. Both research and theory suggest that the skills, values and knowledge associated with social work can make an important contribution to the development of forms of practice conducive to social inclusion and integration, and therefore to crime prevention. We should not leave the warmongers in undisputed possession of the field.

CHAPTER 11

Social Exclusion and Social Work: Policy, Practice and Research

Juliet Cheetham and Roger Fuller

A striking paradox of the concept of social exclusion is its ability to attract the interest of politicians, social scientists, managers of social policy and, as this publication suggests, social workers. It is no mean achievement to bring together, in apparent mutual understanding, people whose interests and responsibilities, although they may appear to occupy a common territory, often diverge. This inclusive potential is useful if it encourages shared debate and the common pursuit of complex problems even though, to the distaste of some, this is brought about by avoiding the harsher and more contentious vocabulary of poverty, disadvantage and inequality, realities which are the daily experience of most users of social work. But there are risks too, especially for social work, if an all-embracing and imprecise concept encourages grandiose thinking about the ends and means of policy and practice. A glimpse of such grand thinking can be found in the National Institute for Social Work's briefing paper *Social Exclusion, Civil Society and Social Work* which asserts that 'in central and eastern Europe, social workers play an important role in the redefinition of relationships between individuals, independent organisations and the state: the Civil Society' (NISW, 1996: 1). This chapter therefore proposes to explore, albeit briefly, the scope of the concept of social exclusion, its strengths for social work and social work research, and what might be done to maximise the benefits of thought and analysis within this framework.

Social exclusion: definitions and impact

Some accounts of social exclusion make it sound familiar territory for social work and social policy. In the *Official Journal of the European Union,* Tiemann (1993, para 352/13) states that:

> social exclusion affects individuals, groups of people and geographical areas. Social exclusion can be seen, not just in levels of income, but also matters such as health, education, access to services, housing and debt. Phenomena which result from social exclusion therefore include: the resurgence of homelessness, urban crises, ethnic tension, rising long term unemployment and persistent high levels of poverty.

Holman's account (Chapter 6) of some features of Easterhouse are living examples of all this. The ESRC (1995) and the EC Targeted Socio-Economic Research Programme (1994–96) extend this description by encouraging exploration of the context of social exclusion. For example, the ESRC which has adopted 'social integration and exclusion' as one of its major thematic priorities describes the purpose of this theme as 'to understand the major societal processes whereby individuals are integrated into, or excluded from, society … to address the causes and implications of divisions within society'. The accompanying commentary is thoroughly inclusive in its invitation to social scientists to explore the structural dynamics of social exclusion – class, 'race', age and gender – the mechanisms of the labour market, political processes, the nature of communities and their cohesion and the role of individuals and institutions in promoting social integration.

This is echoed, on a larger canvas, in the brief of the EC Targeted Socio-Economic Research Programme which aims 'to study how far the actual processes of European integration (single market, economic and monetary union, world context etc.) itself give rise to particular causes of social exclusion and integration'. This programme encourages comparative research and its projects include explorations of homelessness, low wages and unemployment, migration, gender and citizenship.

There are, of course, arguments about the extent to which research under the huge umbrella of social exclusion can go beyond accounts of poverty and relative deprivation such as those of Townsend (1979: 31) who argued that:

> individuals, families and groups in the population can be said to be in poverty when they lack the resources to obtain the kinds of diet, participate in the activities and have the living conditions and amenities which are customary, or at least widely encouraged or approved, in the societies to which they belong. Their resources are so seriously below those commanded by the average individual or family that they are, in effect, excluded from ordinary living patterns, customs and activities.

Certainly the EC policy priorities for combating social exclusion echo strategies of various earlier 'wars against poverty'. For example, the European Commission (1994a) argues that 'preventing and combating social exclusion calls for an overall mobilisation of efforts and combination of both economic and social measures'. The problems also have to be tackled by a partnership between a range of social actors and agencies which helps to define a role for non-governmental organisations which occupy an important place in the EU's approach to social policy. Participation in the decision-making process is also a central aim of policies against social exclusion (Commission, 1993a: 47). Perhaps what is different now is the extent to which contemporary political rhetoric reaffirms the essential union of agencies which must combat social exclusion. In the words of Tony Blair, 'joined up problems require joined up solutions', an affirmation which is expressed again in the government's consultative paper on the NHS *Our Healthier Nation* (Department of Health, 1998) 'connected problems require joined up solutions', and in this paper's insistence that social exclusion is both a cause and effect of health inequalities.

Different too is the greater analytical focus on exclusion as a process rather than a state, which carries with it the emphasis on the extent to which for some poverty is a transitory phenomenon. For example, Walker (1997: 48) has shown that:

typically the poor have been contrasted with the non-poor as if the two groups comprised fixed classes in a hierarchically organised society. While class continues to influence life chances, it is equally true that many poor people swap places with the non-poor... As a consequence the proportion of the European population who experience a shortfall in resources is far greater than indicated by much cited poverty rates. On the other hand, the number of people who are condemned to a life time of penury is thankfully considerably smaller than one might guess by taking the same poverty rates at face value.

Walker goes on to argue that:

in the more immediate future, reconceptualising poverty and exclusion as processes rather than states will ... result in a better understanding of the nature of the problems to be addressed. It also opens the door to policy strategies that are proactive and preventive rather than reactive and ameliorative (1997: 71).

Elsewhere Walker has illustrated some responses to different kinds of poverty which take account of its likely context and duration. Most serious of all, of course, are long or repeated spells of poverty:

in which families lose the dignity that comes with self-determination as they find their best efforts are continually thwarted and their coping strategies are pushed beyond the acceptable, perhaps to such an extent that the locus of control shifts from the family to external social agencies. Social exclusion, in such cases, is a destination on a journey through poverty (1995: 127).

There are clear messages in such analyses for social work intervention: social work must do all it can, in collaboration with those experiencing poverty, to minimise its duration and to devote major effort to preventing the exclusion that can come through both individual behaviour and the mechanisms of social control. A social exclusion framework therefore encourages analyses which go beyond descriptions of static stages and which focus on processes.

Social exclusion discourse can also extend beyond the domain of poverty in, as Walker (1995: 103) argues:

the idea of a society ... comprising people bound together by rights and obligations that reflect, and are defined with respect to, a shared moral order. Exclusion is a state of detachment from this model order and can be brought about by many factors, including limited income.

Such thinking finds a place in debates about citizenship and, as Spicker (1997a, 1997b) has shown, is particularly at home in countries which embrace solidarity and fraternity in their everyday political consciousness. For example,

Lister (1990 and Chapter 3) argues that citizenship has to be understood in terms of an ability to participate in a community. When poverty and other kinds of discrimination – race, age or gender – limit that participation its victims do not have full citizenship. This argument goes beyond Marshall's (1950) conception of citizenship as a set of rights and duties and is concerned also with what people are able to do. With this definition citizenship has to be able to affect people's situations directly. All this is echoed in the European Commission's 1993 Paper:

> when we talk about social exclusion we are acknowledging that the problem is no longer simply one of inequity between the top and the bottom of the social scale ... but also one of the distance within society between those who are active members and those who are forced towards the fringes ... we are also highlighting the effects of the way society is developing and the concomitant risk of social disintegration (1993b: 43, quoted by Paul Spicker, 1997b).

Implications for social work research and practice

These broad and process-oriented conceptions of social exclusion constitute an approach close to the heart of social work, which has a long tradition of seeing individuals and families as members of local networks and influenced by wider environments, and whose practitioners have traditionally been encouraged to think in holistic terms (Richmond, 1917; Hollis, 1964; Pincus and Minahan, 1973; Specht and Vickery, 1977; CCETSW, 1989; Davies, 1997). This encouragement has not always, of course, had an equal impact on social work practice, which has seen fluctuations in its focus on individuals and on their environment. These fluctuations have reflected both political and intellectual fashions, but a central continuing theme has been the relationship between individual experience and its social context. Given, too, that the problems faced by users of social work services are commonly structural in origin but experienced individually, social workers are well-placed to respond to the pleas of Williams (Chapter 2) for an interrogation of traditional boundaries between the public and the private, and of Lister (Chapter 3) for efforts to promote the citizenship of marginalised groups.

A social exclusion canvas also encourages questions about social and political goals, for example, the best means of pursuing solidarity, fraternity and community; and the meaning of inclusion in families whose forms are now in the process of rapid change, partly for demographic reasons. Although all this may seem a far cry from contemporary preoccupations with targeted care packages and cognitive behavioural change programmes for offenders, the purpose, ethics and ultimate effectiveness of such activities must take account of these larger issues. Smith (Chapter 10) has outlined an intriguing and challenging social work agenda within such a framework.

These comments would seem to indicate a potentially close affinity between the charter of professional social work and the struggle against social exclusion, and historically we would argue that this is so. However, social work must acknowledge the arguments, glimpsed in several of the foregoing chapters, for the minutiae of practice to avoid the tendencies which have all too often made social work a bureaucratised and insensitive exercise in people-processing, an impression reinforced, if Beresford and Wilson (Chapter 8) are correct, by the not infrequent use within social work of negative or deficit vocabulary to describe users and by certain constructions of the term social exclusion itself. Such tendencies, some argue, may have increased as the care management role in social work has become more pronounced and direct contact with users de-emphasised. There are powerful arguments here, notably in the chapters by Holman and Lister, for social work to rediscover its neighbourhood and community locus (see below).

It is not at present clear how far social exclusion and inclusion consciously affect the day to day policies and goals of social work, although they appear often enough as part of the vocabulary of the published policy documents of many local authorities. However, perhaps partly in an attempt to attract favourable attention from research funders, social exclusion certainly features as part of the language of social work and social policy research. This was clear in the 1996 Research Assessment Exercise (RAE) through which the UK Higher Education Funding Councils judge the quality of university research. In the 1996 RAE there were 66 social work and social policy submissions from British universities, with social exclusion being cited on the research agenda of about half of these institutions' programmes. Typically this would appear in the form 'social exclusion and X', with 'X' ranging across the panoply of social policy and social work research preoccupations – from addictions to youth justice via dementia and imprisonment, and from employment and migration to women's studies. On further analysis, social exclusion as a research agenda incorporating linked studies was much rarer, perhaps featuring in not more than ten submissions; and in only two or three cases was there a clear research programme with this theme. If the concept is a useful one can it go beyond some kind of filing tray for rather vaguely linked interests? Can social work make use of the concept in a constructive research agenda which is linked to policy and practice?

There are some encouraging signs that it can and that social exclusion can be relevant to contemporary social work in many different contexts. Ensuing sections of this chapter sketch some possible directions for a social work, with its accompanying research agenda, which is informed by the analyses of social exclusion presented in this book.

Social exclusion, social work and communities

As we have seen, the concept of social exclusion can shape a policy agenda and not simply be a framework for research. The idea of 'joined up solutions' is reminiscent of community work and community development programmes which, in the last two decades or so, have been largely absent from social work preoccupations. The fashion for well-planned, task-centred work with individuals, for targeted intervention for those 'most in need' – in part a reaction to the disillusion with the rather ill-defined and grandiose community programmes of the 1960s – has not encouraged work with communities. An integrated analysis, which connects people with their environments has not, of course, been totally absent from the recent social work agenda and may be seen, for example, in the work of family centres. It may also be seen, m contentiously, in the commitment made by social work educators and otʰᵉɪ spokespersons for the profession to anti-discriminatory practice. The part played by discrimination against particular groups in the dynamics of exclusion is a commonplace, and the efforts of social work to highlight anti-discriminatory practice need now to extend to the evaluation of the impact of these endeavours. So far, as Cheetham and Deakin (1997: 440) note, much of the writing on this subject 'has been assertive rather than analytical and lacking robust theoretical and conceptual underpinning'.

Overall, however, British social work, for all the rhetoric of anti-discrimination, empowerment and partnership, has not recently devoted much attention to intervention at the community level. It has relied instead on closer co-ordination with other professional groups – health, education and a plethora of voluntary organisations. At its best this collaborative approach reflects the holism implicit in social exclusion analyses and can bring many positive benefits for service users. These collaborative lessons, which have not been achieved without pain (Hallett, 1995), are a promising context for a reawakened interest in community approaches.

Contemporary examples, few though they are, have lessons to learn from the community development projects of the 1960s and 1970s when government, social workers, researchers and a few citizens tried to transform local communities through injections of cash, self-help and participative politics (Marris and Rein, 1974). The excitement and genuine optimism of the 1960s about the opportunity for regeneration and reform were eventually heavily diluted with disillusion about the feasibility of the objectives, the practicality of evaluative research in such contexts, and the seeming inevitability of passionate ideological disputes.

One example where serious lessons are claimed to have been learnt is the *Communities that Care* project. This is a community-based preventive programme developed initially in the United States, and now sponsored by the Joseph Rowntree Foundation in the UK, involving the old-established principles of community development and incorporating strategies which are strongly research-based. These take account of longitudinal studies of need and vulnerability and local area studies of community strengths and problems. The purpose is to make systematic use of knowledge about risk and protective factors to target individuals, families, schools and communities through a holistic prevention programme. In tune with social exclusion analyses *Communities that Care* 'target multiple problems with multiple solutions and ... make it possible for existing services to be refocused as part of a multi-agency strategy' (Joseph Rowntree Foundation 1997: 25). Monitoring and evaluation are integral to this programme, with a focus on both process and outcomes. The intention is that over a two to three year period an outcome evaluation should show what change has been achieved through focusing on the targeted risk factors and protective factors. In the longer term, communities should look for changes in the incidence of the four problem behaviours which are the particular concern of *Communities that Care*: school failure, school age pregnancy, youth crime and drug abuse.

A further example of community intervention which is likely shortly to be found in Britain also comes from the US. This is based on the experience of the Comprehensive Community Initiatives (CCIs) (Connell et al., 1995). These are neighbourhood-based projects that seek improved outcomes for individuals and families, as well as improvements in neighbourhood circumstances, by working across social, economic and physical sectors, with strong local involvement. The first point to note in these initiatives is the existence of energetic, multi-disciplinary and focused efforts to work in carefully identified communities towards early, immediate and long-term outcomes. There are therefore reasonably clear components to evaluate. The second point of interest is that the evaluation of CCIs is rooted in theories of change – or put more simply, 'how and why an initiative works' (Weiss, 1995) – which underpin the initiatives' activities. These theories of change echo the theories and analyses of social inclusion.

The evaluation of the CCIs is also notable for demanding that the same rigour and creativity is brought to the analysis of the initiative's ongoing activities as to the measurement of their expected outcomes. In short, and perhaps rather unusually for contemporary American social work research, the focus is on both process and outcomes. This wide-ranging research agenda requires a variety of designs and methods which can attempt to capture the complexity of community interventions which posit that improvements in residents' well-being can be achieved through their involvement in local affairs, the increased social capital of the neighbourhood and improvement in social services that are provided locally.

A further example of interest in community approaches can be found in the broad range of activities included in crime prevention (Raynor et al., 1994; Smith, 1995) which aim to reduce opportunities for criminal behaviour and provide some environmental improvement, together with the encouragement of positive local initiatives, for example new, legitimate leisure activities. Here the emphasis on crime as a real social problem is a significant departure from the community development projects of the 1960s and 1970s which, fearful of being seen as a means of regulating rather than empowering the poor, avoided engagement with crime, despite its being a powerful restraint on local solidarity and community cohesion. Smith (1995) has described some early UK ventures which encourage further experimentation, particularly when they involve the co-ordinated efforts of several agencies in a context which accepts the cultural, social and economic causes of crime. There is now a strong case for crime prevention not to be seen just as the property of a few enthusiasts but as an essential element of good social work in criminal justice. This could include youth work, fine default and debt counselling, help with alcohol and drug problems, the improvement of local facilities, educational, recreational and employment programmes and supported accommodation projects. Such interventions, recognising that crime has multiple causes, provide an opportunity to link serious social analysis (some would argue via theories of social exclusion) with well thought out help. It is an example of work with people who, it is sometimes argued, are so socially excluded as to be 'marginal', with this marginality being both a cause and effect of deviance.

Social exclusion and community care

Community care, which aims to maintain people in their own homes or at least in community-based residential establishments instead of hospital, clearly has some kind of inclusive objectives. With some groups of people, particularly those with learning disabilities, the pursuit of 'normalisation' is intended to promote ordinary lives in mainstream society for people who may often be excluded (Wolfensberger and Tullman, 1990). Experience shows that these inclusive aspirations are hard to achieve. Small group homes, day care provision and services whose specialist nature means they can cater for special needs are also exclusive in marking out their residents and participants as different from the majority population, sometimes victims of stigma and discrimination. Why should old people, or any distinctive group, be cared for together? Does this promote cohesion or exclusion? It seems that some of those encouraged into residential or day care to ease their loneliness and isolation in single person households fear and resent what can seem unnatural inclusion. There is an important and subtle research agenda which tracks the chosen and enforced inclusion and exclusion experienced by those who use a variety of welfare provision and those who do not. What realistically can be done to make more ordinary, more accepted and less visible the regimes of residential and group care?

Social exclusion and child care

Within child care there has been since the 1950s and 1960s a major effort both to reduce the number of children taken into public care and, when this occurs, to try and ensure the more 'ordinary' life that can be found within foster homes rather than residential establishments. In the UK virtually all large residential child care institutions have been closed with smaller, homely establishments being a policy objective. This is not uncontentious, particularly since it is argued that there can be tensions between providing establishments large enough to support the specialist staff which may be needed for increasingly disturbed and difficult children and providing homely and continuous care for this particular population (Sinclair and Gibbs, 1996).

Recent policy has sought a shift from an overwhelming emphasis on child abuse investigation towards 'children in need'. Research had shown (for example, Gibbons et al., 1995) that the major efforts and resources which were devoted to identifying children at risk of abuse did not bring in their wake the help for families which might reduce such risks and which would seem an appropriate response to the often desperate levels of disadvantage the enquiries revealed; and that for too many families the disturbance and harm caused by the investigation appeared not to be justified in that they were not included on at-risk registers. Such a change in emphasis is widely interpreted as a move towards more preventive practices, whose impact remains to be seen. Preventive work, something of a holy grail for social work (Hardiker et al., 1991; Fuller, 1992), has clear relevance to a social exclusion analysis. If social work can make a serious impact, through early intervention, on the kinds of problems which lead to children becoming enmeshed in the care system, with all its well-documented damaging consequences, then an important avenue towards social work fulfilling an inclusionary mission is opened up. Expectation here should be sobered by the consideration that social work with children has often in the past seen benign intentions create the very exclusion which social workers have tried to forestall, and (less importantly) that the effectiveness of prevention is notoriously hard to establish.

Relevant here, however, is the contemporary policy insistence that children looked after in the public care system should receive high standards of education, social and health care, and preparation for independence – in other words that their status should, at the very least, not entail a pathway to exclusion. This is reflected in the Department of Health's *Looking after Children* project (Ward, 1995), a system of monitoring children's progress – with them, their families, and their carers – which has a substantial research base and history. The assessment takes account of what are thought, on the basis of research evidence, to be age-appropriate needs, behaviour and targets. No doubt in future decades these will appear a curious product of history; now they can be seen as an attempt to provide a standard of care designed to ensure that children looked after by local authorities do not suffer in comparison with their peers.

Social exclusion and young offenders

Arrangements for dealing with young offenders are a further arena for policies which attempt to combat the stigma and exclusion which accompany some decisions made by youth courts or children's hearings. First and foremost, of course, are the attempts to resist any forms of institutional care, particularly that which has been designed especially for offenders. It has also been argued that supervision orders or any measures which entwine young people and their families with the domain and bureaucracy of social service or social work departments can also be potentially exclusionary. This is because a young person who continues to get into trouble, and to attract the attention of the police and welfare agencies, may accumulate, early in his or her life, a history of 'welfare' interventions, for example, intermediate treatment, which are seen as using up some of the tariff of community-based penalties at sentencers' or other decision makers' disposal.

At one extreme such arguments have prompted responses which are determinedly 'non-responses' in that a decision is made, following some crime or misdemeanour, to eschew formal intervention with the child or his or her family. They may be offered, on a voluntary basis, a variety of services, for example, advice, counselling, clubs and leisure activities which it is thought will be supportive. It is, however, up to the family to accept these or not. The price of this 'radical non-intervention', which keeps a young person off the tariff ladder, may be that little real help is taken up. This kind of stance, in which official agencies note problems but choose to deal with them lightly, usually by referral elsewhere, goes beyond attempts to ration resources logically by targeting people most in need. It is based on an assumption that the very process of involvement with a statutory agency has potentially damaging, albeit unintended, consequences. Some of these may lead to various forms of exclusion, the most traumatic example being periods spent in institutions. It is said too that the labelling of individuals as 'official' problem people can result in stigma. This might include various kinds of observation or surveillance of behaviour, or an expectation, for example in school, of failure or poor performance.

Smith's chapter carries this analysis much further forward and, in addition to straightforward examples of 'including' social work measures, offers some visionary, even revolutionary systems of criminal justice and social policy which would diminish exclusion. Some of this may be ahead of contemporary research, but it deserves its best attentions.

The sad paradox of such strategies, which here are only briefly and rather crudely described, is that social work appears to believe that help which is intended to be inclusive in its ends and means may in fact work towards the exclusion of the very people who are the object of the intervention. How far this is a reality, and how far it is a consequence of demoralisation of social work which has been subject to so much fierce criticism, fair and unfair, in the last decades, is difficult to judge. The fashion for this theory of exclusion via welfare has waxed and waned and its research basis is slight. While it is certainly possible to track the progress through tariff systems of substantial numbers of troublesome young people whose troubles become the object of official attention, it is virtually impossible to compare their overall fate with those not subject to any form of official attention or help.

Minimising exclusion

There is, however, enough known about effective and less effective practice, and about users' preferences, for social workers and their managers to think hard about the way in which their services and efforts may be exclusive. Some exclusion may be unavoidable, for example children may have to be received into care, with all its excluding potential. Recognising this, the social work task then is to work energetically towards 'normalising' the experience of people who might be isolated from their families and communities by making the barriers between ordinary and institutional life as permeable as possible and by encouraging maximum contact between parents and children. Easing the transitions and promoting the independence of people who have experienced some form of isolation from mainstream society is a further crucial responsibility.

The research agenda in all this includes identifying those features of social work which are perceived as bringing about stigma, as a gateway to other unwelcome attention, or as erecting various hurdles between those thought of as ordinary citizens and those who are the recipients of welfare. A small but striking example of social work's potentially excluding aura can be found in its offices and reception areas and systems. There have been attempts to make these easy to locate and welcoming, softening the officialdom of a welfare agency by, crucially, staff's demeanour but also through attention paid to waiting areas. But there are many examples too of reception systems which at best are discouraging and at worst repelling. No-one happily sits in dingy, uncomfortable waiting rooms, pressing the anonymous bell for the glass door to be opened a crack by a hassled receptionist who has many other tasks. Anyone who is screwing courage to the sticking place to approach a welfare agency could find this environment an overwhelming obstacle. The forms, information leaflets, assessment schedules and bureaucratic letters can also be deterring, particularly when no attention is paid to the needs of people with communication difficulties or those who do not speak English.

Resources which come in the shape of bricks and mortar, places in which you live or stay for part of the day, may present opportunities, asylum, protection and a place where isolated people can be brought into some kind of society; but such places can isolate, stigmatise or simply encourage a dependence on systems which do not fit well in a world which turns on individual effort. Prisons and large residential institutions such as psychiatric hospitals are obvious examples but small children's homes and homes for elderly people can also encourage, unwittingly, unhelpful dependence. Small and rewarding societies can thrive within such large systems but they are unlikely to be the establishments of choice; and they are in many cases not a helpful preparation for a more mixed and heterogeneous world. 'Inclusive' activities are therefore on the social work agenda, for example, throughcare in penal establishments, preparation for independence for young people leaving residential care, mainstream community links for people living in residential homes. There are imaginative attempts at all this but the problems confronted are enormous (Booth, 1985; Stein and Carey, 1986). There will continue to be attempts to make transitions easier and barriers more permeable – another promising arena for practice linked to research.

Choosing inclusion

Most of the argument and illustration so far has assumed clear agreement about the merits and means of inclusion but this consensus cannot be assumed for either individuals or categories of user. Homelessness may seem the lesser evil compared with enforced group living; and the conformity which may be the price of inclusion may seem a poor bargain. There are obvious dangers in an insensitive inclusive agenda. Some groups, particularly disabled people (Fisher, Chapter 7), are clear and articulate about what they want: the ordinary necessities of a fulfilling life; work, income, access to mainstream education and training; in short a place in the ordinary world. In this vision it is social work's obligation to enable rather than provide directly.

There are, however, other less comfortable and more contentious examples. It is possible to argue that social workers and others who have responsibility for people at risk of exclusion should encourage them into certain pathways – for example, education, leisure, and accommodation – which will diminish isolation and wider exclusion. Such decisions are commonly made for children and young people, although hopefully in consultation with them. Pressures may also be brought upon people in institutions to set foot in a different world of supported accommodation and community care. This may be the product of policies which have not been constructed by social work but with which it is largely in accord. The price of this 'enforced inclusion' for some people may be considerable. Far more studies are needed to explore the conditions for satisfying inclusion into ordinary society for people who spend substantial periods in residential care.

Another important policy matter, which is far too little illuminated by research, concerns the extent to which people who have some shared identity because of language, culture or some common problems should have services and associations designed particularly for them. It is sometimes assumed, with the backing of service users, that such arrangements will provide a more welcoming and helpful environment than mainstream, generic services. This has been a live and contentious issue in planning education and social services for ethnic minorities, and here the debates have been characterised more by ideology and passion than evidence about the outcomes of different systems. For example, in education it has been argued that separate schools for religious groups tend to reinforce isolation and tension (Swann, 1985); it is also said, and there is some evidence of this in the USA and elsewhere (for example, Kirp, 1982), that such a system of education, by giving some security to groups who may feel marginalised, increases their confidence and ability to move easily between the familiarity of an ethnic group and the wider world. Again, within social work this is a subject which deserves subtle research of preference, process and outcome.

Social exclusion and the research act

We have thus far discussed future agendas for social work and research in the light of the ways of seeing opened up by the concept of social exclusion. It remains to acknowledge that at the same time there are serious cognate implications for the ways in which research is conducted. For if the practice of social work can be said to exhibit tendencies to demean, to weaken the sense of self, to label as different, so too can the practice of research. At one time, when researchers considered their obligations to 'subjects', it might have been thought sufficient to honour, perhaps in minimalist ways, the stipulations in all the codes of practice concerning informed consent and guarantees of anonymity and confidentiality. This is no longer straightforwardly so, not least because of the questioning of terms like 'subject' prompted by the presence among the ranks of researchers of people who may themselves be disabled, be a member of an ethnic minority, or have grown up in care. This can be a salutary reminder of the connectedness of the once hermetically sealed worlds of academe and the socially marginalised. The continuing rarity of such reminders should lead to a recasting of the relation between researcher and researched, and a fuller understanding of the power differential which may be implicit in the research act.

In the last two decades social work research has, very broadly, moved from an emphasis on studies of need to one on evaluation. In part the focus on evaluation, since the 1980s, has been at the behest of senior policy-makers – a top-down phenomenon – albeit one sufficiently influenced by a consumerist perspective to place increasing emphasis on obtaining user views. Increasingly, however, there has developed alongside this a bottom-up critique, sometimes user-led, undertaken in an emancipatory spirit, and seeking to foreground the perspectives of service users, or of other excluded, marginalised or oppressed groups. As a form of words, 'doing research with...' has to some extent displaced 'doing research on...' At the same time, there has been exploration of different ways of involving service users more meaningfully in research (see, for example, Wilson, 1995; Stalker, 1998). These have included increased attention to the manner in which users are sought as respondents, with a more scrupulous concern for their capacity to refuse to take part; undertakings to circulate research results to respondents in accessible form; inviting users to be part of research advisory groups, or finding other, more appropriate ways of seeking user advice on the conduct of the research; enlisting users' help in the design of instruments; utilising users as interviewers, as validators of findings, as disseminators; involving users in the shaping of research agendas or framing of research proposals. At the end of the spectrum may be a situation where the power relation is reversed, and a researcher undertakes a study at the behest of a user-led organisation (for example, People First, 1994).

While all of this may offer some kind of protection against the risk that the processes of research will themselves be exclusionary or contribute to an excluded identity, there are a number of caveats to be made. Clearly some of these procedures may be operated in a tokenistic or utilitarian manner rather than out of a desire genuinely to include. User 'representatives' may not in fact be very representative, but exhibit rather a bias towards the articulate or activist. Users may experience the process of involvement in research as one of co-option, or at best feel that the fora in which they are invited to make their views known are alien and uncomfortable. Most particularly, Beresford and Wilson (Chapter 8) sound a clarion call for excluded groups to be involved in discussions of exclusion, but also issue a warning note: they may not, for a variety of reasons, wish to be included, not least because however fully users are involved there is no guarantee that the research and the way it is used will be in their interests. What is in it for them?

There are underlying questions here about who owns research and who should. In an allegedly post-modern world where the traditional purposes of research as a detached and 'expert' shedding of light are questioned, where it seems problematic to see it as a public good, and where everything is 'socially constructed' (Hacking, 1997), it is tempting to view research as primarily a means of letting previously silent voices be heard. And such voices are being heard more and more, some relatively loud and clear (disabled people, psychiatric survivors, increasingly children), others more muted (older people, those with learning disabilities). For some, too, an appropriate model for social work research is research undertaken from a feminist or anti-racist standpoint, as interestingly discussed by Trinder (1996). As Gouldner (1968) remarked in a much collected essay long ago, confessions of partisan commitment may be good for the soul, but are not necessarily a tonic for the mind. However politically attractive as a means of practising what is preached, adopting users as co-researchers or relabelling them as co-authors may result in an abdication of the intellectual and moral responsibilities of analysis and authorship (Geertz, 1988). While undeniable progress has been made in understanding of the methods and practicalities of user involvement in research, and much recent research has been the stronger for it, there are debates still to be properly developed about the politics of so doing.

Conclusion

Academics and researchers tend now to be seen as a rather gloomy group – carping at the deficiencies of contemporary conceptual analysis and pessimistic about the impact of emerging social policies. We have decided, with what degree of justification time will decide, to strike a different and more optimistic note. We believe that, under the umbrella of social inclusion, intellectual and policy interests are interacting today more closely than for several decades. We also believe that social work – understood broadly to include all the public, voluntary and private agencies and groups concerned with individual and community welfare – has a significant place in this agenda.

A degree of support for this optimism can be found in the prospectus for New Labour's Social Exclusion Unit (1997). In this we are reminded, in refreshingly simple terms, that:

> social exclusion is a shorthand label for what can happen when individuals or areas suffer from a combination of linked problems such as unemployment, poor skills, low incomes, poor housing, high crime environments, bad health and family breakdown.

We are told too that, while the unit will address 'the long term causes of social exclusion', it has in the first instance three key tasks: to reduce the scale of truancy and school exclusion, and to find better solutions for those who have been excluded; to reduce the extent of street living; and to develop integrated and sustainable approaches to the problems of the worst housing estates. On the agenda too are the identification of key preventive interventions with children and young people; options for improving access to services for low income areas or individuals; and probing aspects of exclusion which disproportionately affect particular ethnic minority groups. The unit, which is interdisciplinary and cross-departmental, will, it is explained, draw extensively on outside expertise and research, listen to the views of organisations and individuals with experience of dealing with social exclusion, seek out good practice and encourage its dissemination, and be 'outward-facing and open'.

The ingrained scepticism of commentators must be given its due: political energies may prove evanescent or illusory, identities of interest between governments and welfare reformers are rarely total, and with such a huge canvas there could be many disappointments. Before these crowd in, however, let us look at the opportunities. That (all too large) part of the world which is the concern of the Social Exclusion Unit is also the world of social work; and there seems now to be an invitation for it to be proactive, open and enquiring. Social work can be proactive by holding firmly to its role as a witness to the circumstances and sufferings of excluded people, and the ways in which policy and practice can enhance or diminish their exclusion. Social work needs to be open and enquiring because it is certain that its excluding potential will continue to attract attention and criticism, both fair and unfair. The natural defensive response can be diminished by social work's own commitment to examining through all kinds of enquiry, from practitioner research (Fuller and Petch, 1995) to large externally funded studies, the ways it can maximise the inclusion of the people it serves. All this may be done in many different ways but must ensure that the voices of some of the greatest experts – excluded people themselves –

are heard in those arenas which can affect policy: the media, community and political groups, and through research.

Social work's observation and recording role has a long history, perhaps starting with the contributions made by the ancestors of contemporary social workers to nineteenth century enquiries into the conditions of the poor. And, as Sinfield has observed, this role was recognised by at least one reforming politician, Clement Attlee, who wrote in 1920:

> Social investigation is a particular form of social work … it is not possible for the ordinary rank and file of social workers to hope to rival skilled investigators, but each one can take his part by cultivating habits of careful observation and analysis of the pieces of social machinery that come under his notice (cited by Sinfield, 1969: 53).

During the previous Conservative administration pleas for the poor or analyses of the breakdown of social and civic relations were frequently dismissed as 'whinging', or sustaining a fiction of 'society' when in reality there were only families and individuals. Serious and subtle social analysis is now encouraged, and social work can play its part.

References

Abel-Smith, B. and Townsend, P. (1965) *The Poor and the Poorest*, London: Bell and Sons.

ADSW (1997) *Social Work into the Millennium: Critical Issues for Social Work Services in Scotland*, Glasgow: Association of Directors of Social Work.

Ahmad, V. and Atkin, K. (1996) *Race and Community Care*, Buckingham: Open University Press.

Alcock, P. (1997) *Understanding Poverty*, Second edition, Basingstoke: Macmillan.

Alexander, M. J. and Mohanty, C. T. (eds.) (1997) *Feminist Genealogies, Colonial Legacies, Democratic Futures*, New York: Routledge.

Arnold, J. and Jordan, B. (1996) 'Poverty', in M. Drakeford and M. Vanstone (eds.) *Beyond Offending Behaviour*, Aldershot: Arena.

Ashdown, P. (1997) Speech on 5.2. 97, *reported in the Independent* 6.2.97.

Ashworth, K. and Walker, R. (1991) 'The Role of Time in the Definition and Measurement of Poverty', Loughborough University Working Paper 154, Loughborough: CRSP.

ATD Fourth World, (1996) *Talk With Us, Not At Us: How to Develop Partnerships Between Families in Poverty and Professionals*, London: ATD Fourth World

Audit Commission for Local Authorities and the National Health Service in England and Wales (1995), *Paying the Piper: People and Pay Management in Local Government*, London: HMSO.

Auletta, K. (1982) *The Underclass*, New York: Random House.

Bagguley, P. and Mann, K. (1992) 'Idle Thieving Bastards? Scholarly Representations of the "Underclass"', *Work, Employment and Society* 6 (1): 113–126.

Baldwin, D., Coles, B. and Mitchell, W. (1997) in R. MacDonald (ed.), *Youth, the 'Underclass' and Social Exclusion*, London: Routledge.

Barron, D (1996) *A Price to be Born*, Harrogate: Mencap Northern Division.

Barry, M. and Sidaway, R. (forthcoming) 'Empowerment Through Partnership' in W. Shera and L. Wells (eds.) *Empowerment Practice in Social Work: Developing Richer Conceptual Foundations*, New York: Colombia University Press.

Bauböck, R. (1994) *Transnational Citizenship: Membership and Rights in International Migration*, Aldershot: Edward Elgar.

Bauman, Z. (1997) *Times Literary Supplement*, 24 1.97: 4.

Bebbington, A. and Miles, J. (1989) 'The Background of Children who Enter Local Authority Care', *British Journal of Social Work,* Vol. 19, No. 5, 349–368.

Becker, S. (1997) *Responding to Poverty,* London: Longman.

Beres, Z. and Wilson, G. (1997) 'Essential Emotions: the Place of Passion in a Feminist Network', *Non Profit Management and Leadership*, 8, 2: 171–182.

Beresford, P. (1995) 'Voices From The Sharp End: Service Users and the Future of the Welfare State', *Community Care*, 6–11 January: 20–21.

Beresford, P. (1997) 'The Last Social Division?: Revisiting the Relationship Between Social Policy, its Producers and Consumers', in M. May, E. Brunsdon and G. Craig (eds.) *Social Policy Review* 9: 203–226.

Beresford, P. and Campbell, J. (1994) 'Disabled People, Service Users, User Involvement and Representation', *Disability And Society*, Volume 9, No 3: 315–325.

Beresford, P. and Croft, S. (1993) *Citizen Involvement: A practical guide for change*, Basingstoke, Macmillan.

Beresford, P. and Croft, S. (1995), 'It's Our Problem Too!: Challenging the Exclusion of Poor People from Poverty Discourse', *Critical Social Policy*, Issue 44/45, Autumn: 75–95.

133

Beresford, P. and Croft, S. (1997) 'Postmodernity and the Future of Welfare: Whose Critiques, Whose Social Policy?', in J. Carter (ed.), *Postmodernity and the Fragmentation of Welfare: A contemporary Social Policy?*, London: Routledge.

Beresford, P. and Turner, M (1997) *It's Our Welfare: Report of the Citizens' Commission on the Future of the Welfare State*, London: National Institute for Social Work.

Beresford, P., Stalker, K. and Wilson, A. (1997) *Speaking for Ourselves: A Bibliography*, London: Open Services Project in association with the Social Work Research Centre, University of Stirling.

Beresford, P., Green, D, Lister, R. and Woodard, K. (1998) *Poverty First Hand: Poor People Speak for Themselves*, London: Child Poverty Action Group.

Berghman, J. (1995) 'Social Exclusion in Europe: Policy Context and Analytical Framework', in G. Room (ed.), *Beyond the Threshold: the Measurement and Analysis of Social Exclusion*, Bristol: The Policy Press.

Booth, C. (1889) *The Life and Labour of the People,* London: Williams and Northgate.

Booth, T. (1985) *Home Truths: Old People's Homes and the Outcome of Care,* Aldershot: Gower.

Bottoms, A. E. (1989) 'The Place of the Probation Service in the Criminal Justice System', In Central Council of Probation Committees, *The Madingley Papers II,* Cambridge: University of Cambridge.

Bottoms, A. E. and Stelman, A. (1988) *Social Inquiry Reports*, Aldershot: Wildwood House.

Brah, A. (1996) *Cartographies of Diaspora*, London: Routledge.

Braithwaite, J. (1989) *Crime, Shame and Reintegration*, Cambridge: Cambridge University Press.

Braithwaite, J. (1995) 'Reintegrative Shaming, Republicanism and Policy', in H. D. Barlow (ed.) *Crime and Public Policy*, Oxford: Westview Press.

Brighouse, S. (1997) *Letter to Social Exclusion Unit, as Chair, UK Coalition Against Poverty*, London, 15 December.

Bulmer, M. and Rees, A. M. (eds.) (1996), *Citizenship Today*, London: UCL Press

Burnside, J. and Baker, N. (ed.) (1994) *Relational Justice: Repairing the Breach*, Winchester: Waterside Press.

Burrows, R. and Loader, B. (eds.) (1994), *Towards a Post-Fordist Welfare State*, London: Routledge.

Campbell, P. (1996), 'The History of the User Movement in the United Kingdom', in Campbell, J. and Oliver, M. (1996), *Disability Politics: Understanding our Past, Changing our Future*, London: Routledge.

T. Heller, J. Reynolds, R. Gomm, R. Muston and S. Pattison (eds.) *Mental Health Matters*, Basingstoke: Macmillan.

Carr-Hill, R. (1995) 'Measurement of User Satisfaction', in G. Wilson (ed.) *Community Care: Asking the Users*, London: Chapman and Hall.

Castles, S. (1994) 'Democracy and Multi-cultural Citizenship: Australian Debates and their Relevance for Western Europe', in R. Bauböck (ed.) *From Aliens to Citizens: Redefining the Status of Immigrants in Europe,* Aldershot: Avebury.

Castles, S. (1996) 'Democracy and Multi-culturalism in Western Europe', *Journal of Area Studies,* 8: 51–76.

Castles, S. and Miller, M. J. (1993) *The Age of Migration: International Population Movements in the Modern World,* Aldershot: Avebury.

CCETSW (1989) *Requirements and Regulations for the Diploma in Social Work,* Paper 30, London: CCETSW.

Channel 4 News (1997) *The Swedish Sterilisation Programme*, 29 August.

Cheetham, J. (1997) *Social Exclusion: A real Research Agenda or a Convenient Label? A Challenge for Social Work Policy and Practice*, Paper to International Conference 'On The Margins: Social Exclusion and Social Work', Stirling: University of Stirling.

Cheetham, J. and Deakin, N. (1997) 'Assessing the Assessment: Some Reflections on the 1996 Higher Education Funding Council's Research Assessment Exercise', *British Journal of Social Work*, 27, 435–442.

Children's Rights Development Unit (1994) *UK Agenda for Children,* London: CRDU.

Christie, N. (1993) *Crime Control as Industry: Towards GULAGS, Western Style?*, London: Routledge.

Christie, N. (1997) 'Four Blocks Against Insight: Notes on the Oversocialization of Criminologists', *Theoretical Criminology*, 1, 1: 13–23.

Clarke, J. and Newman, J. (1997) *The Managerial State*, London: Sage.

Cockburn, C. (1996a) 'Different Together: Women in Belfast', *Soundings*, 2: 32–47.

Cockburn, C. (1996b) 'Mixing it', *Red Pepper,* September: 22–24.

Coles, B. (1995) *Youth and Social Policy: Youth citizenship and Young Careers,* London: UCL Press.

Commission for Racial Equality (1992) *Cautions and Prosecutions*, London: CRE.

Commission of the European Communities (1993a) *European Social Policy – Options for the Union*, Green Paper Cmnd. 93, Luxembourg: European Commission.

Commission of the European Communities (1993b) *Medium Term Action Programme to Counter Exclusion and Promote Solidarity,* Luxembourg: European Commission.

Commission of the European Communities (1994a) *European Social Policy – a Way Forward for the Union,* White Paper Cmnd. 333, Luxembourg: European Commission.

Commission of the European Communities (1994b) *Growth, Competitiveness, Employment: The Challenges and the Way Forward into the 21st Century*, Luxembourg: European Commission.

Connell, J., Kuboch, A., Schon, L. and Weiss, C. (eds.) (1995) *New Approaches to Evaluating Community Initiatives: Concepts, Methods and Contexts*, Washington DC: The Aspen Institute.

Croft, S. and Beresford, P. (1989) 'Time for Social Work to Gain New Confidence', *Social Work Today,* 13 April.

Croft, S. and Beresford, P. (1993a) 'A Poor Show: The Commission on Social Justice', *New Statesman and Society*, 19 March: 23.

Croft, S. and Beresford, P. (1993b) *Getting Involved: A Practical Manual*, London: Open Services Project/Joseph Rowntree Foundation.

CSJ/IPPR (1994) *Social Justice: Strategies for National Renewal*, London: IPPR/Vintage.

Curriculum Development Group (1989) *Welfare Rights in Social Work Education*, London: CCETSW.

Davies, M. (ed.) (1997) *The Blackwell Companion to Social Work,* Oxford: Blackwell.

Dean, H. (1996) 'Who's Complaining? Redress and Social Policy' in M. May, E. Brunsdon and G. Craig (eds.) *Social Policy Review* 8, Kent: Social Policy Association.

Dearden, C. and Becker, S. (1995) *Young Carers: The Facts*, Sutton: Reed Business Publishing/Young Carers Research Group.

Deklerck, J. and Depuydt, A. (1995) 'The Cycle of Integration and Disintegration Applied to Western Society: a Framework for a Fundamental Prevention of Delinquency', Paper to international conference 'Einstein Meets Magritte: an Inter-disciplinary Reflection on Science, Nature, Human Action and Society', V.U.B: Brussels, May-June.

Denney, D (1992) *Racism and anti-racism in Probation*, London: Routledge.

Department of the Environment (1997) *Developing an Integrated Transport Policy*, A Consultation Paper, August, London: Department of the Environment.

Department of Health (1998) *Our Healthier Nation*, London: The Stationery Office.

Depuydt, A. and Deklerck, J. (1997) 'An Integrative Approach to Crime Prevention Based on the Concepts of "Linkedness" and "Integration v. Disintegration"', Paper to conference 'Restorative Justice for Juveniles', K.U. Leuven, May.

Devlin, A. (1995) *Criminal Classes*, Winchester: Waterside Press.

Diba, R. (1996) M*eeting the Costs of Continuing Care: Public Views and Perceptions*, York: York Publishing Services, for Joseph Rowntree Foundation.

Dodd, T. and Hunter, P. (1992) *The National Prison Survey 1991*, London: HMSO.

Dominelli, L. (1997) *Sociology For Social Work*, Basingstoke: Macmillan.

Doyal, L. and Gough, I. (1991) *A Theory of Human Need,* Basingstoke: Macmillan.

Drakeford, M. and Vanstone, M. (1996) 'Introduction', in M. Drakeford and M. Vanstone (eds.) *Beyond Offending Behaviour*, Aldershot: Arena.

Duffy, K. (1995) *Social Exclusion and Human Dignity in Europe*, Background report for the proposed initiative by the Council of Europe, Brussels: CDPS.

Eagleton, T. (1997) 'Spaced out', *London Review of Books*, 24 April: 23.

Esping-Andersen, G. (ed.) (1990) *The Three Worlds of Welfare Capitalism*, Cambridge: Polity Press.

Esping-Anderson, G. (ed.) (1996) *Welfare States in Transition*, London: Sage.

ESRC (1995) *Thematic Priorities,* Economic and Social Research Council.

Etzioni, A. (1997) *The New Golden Rule: Community and Morality in a Democratic Society,* Profile Books.

European Foundation for the Improvement of Living and Working Conditions (1995) *Public Welfare Services and Social Exclusion: The Development of Consumer Oriented Initiatives in the European Union,* Dublin: The Foundation.

Evans, C. (1997) 'Doing it for Ourselves', *Inside Community Care,* 29 May-4 June.

Farrington, D P. (1996) *Understanding and Preventing Youth Crime*, York: Joseph Rowntree Foundation.

Field, F. (1997) Personal communication, 1 July.

FitzGerald, M. (1993) *Ethnic Minorities and the Criminal Justice System*, Royal Commission on Criminal Justice, London: HMSO.

Foucault, M. (1979) *Discipline and Punish*, London: Harmondsworth Penguin.

Fraser, N. (1987) 'Women, Welfare and the Politics of Need Interpretation', *Hypatia*, 2(1): 103–121.

Freedland, J. (1997) Master Race of the Left, *The Guardian*, August 30.

Friedman, M. (1962) *Capitalism and Freedom,* University of Chicago Press.

Fuller, R. (1992) *In Search of Prevention*, Aldershot: Avebury.

Fuller, R. and Petch, A. (1995) *Practitioner Research: the Reflexive Social Worker*, Buckingham: Open University Press.

Galbraith, J. K. (1996) *The Good Society,* London: Sinclair-Stevenson.

Gaventa, J. (1998) 'Poverty, Participation and Social Exclusion in North and South' in A. de Haan and S. Maxwell (eds.) *Poverty and Social Exclusion in North and South,* Vol. 29, No. 1, January, IDS Bulletin: 50–57.

Geertz, C. (1988) *Works and Lives: the Anthropologist as Author*, Oxford: Polity Press.

Gelsthorpe, L. and Raynor, P. (1995) 'Quality and Effectiveness in Probation Officers' Reports to Sentencers', *British Journal of Criminology*, 35, 2, 188–200.

George, M. (1997) 'The Fight to Vote', *Community Care,* 13–19 March.

Gibbons, J., Thorpe, S. and Wilkinson, P. (1990) *Family Support and Prevention*, London: HMSO.

Gibbons, J., Conroy, S. and Bele, C. (1995) *Operating the Child Protection System*, London: HMSO.

Giddens, A. (1991) *Modernity and Self-identity,* Cambridge: Polity Press.

Giddens, A. (1994) *Beyond Left and Right: The Future of Radical Politics*, Cambridge: Polity Press.

Gilligan, C. (1982) *In a Different Voice: Psychological Theory and Women's Development*, Cambridge, Mass: Harvard University Press.

Glasgow College (1997) *Council Housing and Unemployment, Discussion paper No.6, April.* Glasgow: Policy Analysis Research Unit.

Glasgow Regeneration Alliance (1997) *Greater Glasgow Housing Choice Survey 1996,* Glasgow: Glasgow City Council and Scottish Homes.

Goffman, E. (1975) *Asylums*, London: Harmondsworth Penguin.

Gordon, D and Pantazis, C. (eds.) (1997) *Breadline Britain in the 1990s*, Aldershot: Ashgate.

Gould, C. (1988) *Rethinking Democracy*, Cambridge: Cambridge University Press.

Gouldner, A. (1968) 'The Sociologist as Partisan: Sociology and the Welfare State', *American Sociologist*, 3: 103–116.

Green, R. (1997) *Community Action Against Poverty*, Kingsmead: Kabin.

Gruer, L. (1998) Greater Glasgow Health Board Drug Action Team, personal communication.

de Haan, A. (1998) 'Social Exclusion': An Alternative Concept for the Study of Deprivation?' in A. de Haan and S. Maxwell (eds.) *Poverty and Social Exclusion in North and South*, Vol. 29, No. 1, January, IDS Bulletin: 10–19.

Hacking, I. (1997) 'Taking Bad Arguments Seriously: Psychopathology and Social Construction', *London Review of Books* 19, 16: 14–16.

Hall, S. (1996) 'Drifting into a Law and Order Society' in *Criminological Perspectives*, London: Sage.

Hall, S. and Held, D (1989) 'Left and Rights', *Marxism Today,* June, 16–23.

Hallett, C. (1995) *Interagency Co-ordination in Child Protection*, London: HMSO.

Harden, I. (1992) *The Contracting State,* Buckingham: Open University Press.

Hardiker, P., Exton, K. and Barker, M. (1991) *Policies and Practices in Preventive Child Care*, Aldershot: Avebury.

Harrow, J. and Shaw, M. (1992) 'The Manager Faces the Consumer' in L. Willcocks and J. Harrow (eds.) *Rediscovering Public Services Management*, London: McGraw Hill.

Hayek, F.(1944) *The Road to Serfdom,* London: Routledge & Kegan Paul.

Heidensohn, F. (1986) 'Models of Justice: Portia or Persephone? Some Thoughts on Equality, Justice, Gender and Fairness in the Field of Criminal Justice', *International Journal of the Sociology of Law*, 14: 187–98.

Held, D (1995) *Democracy and the Global Order,* Cambridge: Polity Press.

Henderson, P. (1997) *Social Inclusion and Citizenship in Europe:. The Contribution of Community Development*, Den Haag: Combined European Bureau for Social Development.

Henderson, P. (ed.) (1995) *Children and Communities*, London: Pluto Press.

Hewitt, M. (1994), 'Social Policy and the Question of Postmodernism' in R. Page and J. Baldock (eds.) *Social Policy Review 6*, Canterbury: Social Policy Association.

Hollis, F. (1964) *Casework: a Psycho-Social Therapy*, New York: Random House.

Holman, B. (1988a) 'Forum', *Community Care*, 24 November.

Holman, B. (1988b) *Putting Families First*, Macmillan Education.

Holman, B. (1993a) *A New Deal for Social Welfare*, Oxford: Lion Publishing.

Holman, B. (1993b) 'Pulling Together', *The Guardian*, 20 January.

Holman, B. (1997) *FARE Dealing. Neighbourhood Involvement in a Housing Scheme*, Community Development Foundation.

Home Office (1993) *Race and Criminal Justice,* Report from the CCJC Sub-Committee on Race Issues, London: Home Office.

Home Office (1994) *The Ethnic Origins of Prisoners*, Home Office Statistical Bulletin 21/ 94, London: HMSO.

Home Office (1997) *Race and the Criminal Justice System: A Home Office publication under Section 95 of the Criminal Justice Act 1991*, December, London: HMSO.

Hopenhayn, M. (1993) 'Postmodernism and Neoliberalism in Latin America', *The Post Modern Debate in Latin America,* Special Issue boundary 2, 20, 3, 93–109.

Hughes, G. (1996) 'Communitarianism and Law and Order', *Critical Social Policy*, 16(4), 17–41.

Hutton, W. (1995) *The State We're In*, London: Jonathan Cape.

Ingleby Committee (1960), *The Report of the Committee on Children and Young Persons,* Cmnd. 1191, London: HMSO.

IPPR (1997) *Quantitative Survey on Attitudes to Race*, London: IPPR.

Issacs, S. (ed.) (1941) *The Cambridge Evacuation Survey,* London: Methuen.

Jones, C. (1996) 'Anti-Intellectualism and the Peculiarities of British Social Work Education', In N. Parton (ed.) *Social Theory, Social Change And Social Work*, London: Routledge.

Jordan, B. (1975) 'Is the Client a Fellow Citizen?', *Social Work Today,* 30 October.

Jordan, B. (1996) *A Theory of Poverty and Social Exclusion*, Cambridge: Polity Press.

Joseph Rowntree Foundation (1996) 'The Future of Work', *Social Policy Summary 7,* February.

Joseph Rowntree Foundation (1997) *Communities that Care*, York: Joseph Rowntree Foundation.

Keith, M. (1996) 'Criminalisation and Racialization' in J. Muncie, E. McLaughlin and M. Langan (eds.), *Criminological Perspectives*, London: Sage.

Kilbrandon, L. (1964) *Children & Young Persons Scotland*, Cmnd. 2306, Edinburgh: Scottish Home and Health Department.

Kirp, D L. (1982) *Just Schools: the Idea of Racial Equality in American Education,* Berkeley: University of California Press.

Kymlicka, W. and Norman, W. (1994), 'Return of the Citizen', *Ethics,* No 104, January: 352–81.

Lankshear, G. and Giarchi, G. G. (1995) 'Finding out About Consumer Views: an Experiment in the Group Method', in Wilson G. (ed.) *Community Care Asking the Users*, London: Chapman and Hall.

Lansbury, G. (1928) *My Life,* London: Constable.

Lawrie, W. (1996) *The Inclusion of Disabled Children in Schools – Strategies for Success.*

Lechner, N. (1993) 'A Disenchantment called Postmodernism', *The Post Modern Debate in Latin America Special Issue boundary* 2, 20, 3: 122–139.

Leibfried, S. and Pierson, P. (eds.) (1995) *European Social Policy: Between Fragmentation and Integration*, Washington: Brookings Institute.

Leissner, A., Herdman, K. and Davies, E. (1971) *Advice, Guidance and Assistance: a Study of Seven Family Advice Centres.* London: Longman, for The National Children's Bureau.

Lenoir, R. (1974) *Les Exclus: Un Francais Sur Dix*, Paris: Editions de Seuil.

Levitas, R. (1997) 'Discourses of Social Inclusion and Integration: from the European Union to New Labour', Paper presented at the *European Sociological Conference*, University of Essex, August.

Levitas, R. (1996) 'The Concept of Social Exclusion and the New Durkheimian Hegemony', in *Critical Social Policy* No 16 (1), pp. 5–20.

Lindow, V. (1994) *Self-Help Alternatives To Mental Health Services*, London: MIND Publications.

Lipsky, M. (1980) *Street Level Bureaucracy*, New York: Russell Sage Foundation.

Lister, R. (1990) *The Exclusive Society: Citizenship and the Poor*, London: Child Poverty Action Group.

Lister, R. (1997a) *Citizenship: Feminist Perspectives*, Basingstoke: Macmillan.

Lister, R. (1997b) 'Whose Community?', *Community Care*, 29 May – 4 June, 25.

Lister, R. (1998) 'Citizenship on the Margins: Citizenship, Social Work and Social Action', in *European Journal of Social Work*, vol. 1, 1: 5–18.

Lister, R. (in press) 'Citizenship in Action: Citizenship and Community Development in a Northern Ireland Context', *Community Development Journal*.

Lister, R. and Beresford, P. (1991) *Working Together Against Poverty: Involving Poor People in Action Against Poverty*, London: Open Services Project and Department of Applied Social Studies, University of Bradford.

Lloyd, A. (1997) Regina vs Gloucester County Council and The Secretary of State for Health, ex partie Barry (AP) Ruling 20 March.

Mandelson, P. (1997a) *Labour's Next Steps: Tackling Social Exclusion*, lecture delivered to the Fabian Society, 14 August.

Mandelson, P. (1997b) Channel Four News, 14 August.

Mandelson, P. (1997c) 'A Lifeline for Youth', *The Guardian*, 15 August, 17.

Marris, P. and Rein, M. (1974) *Dilemmas of Social Reform*, London: Harmondsworth Penguin.

Marshall, T. H. (1950) *Citizenship and Social Class*, Cambridge: Cambridge University Press.

Martin, J. (1984) *Hospitals in Trouble*, Oxford: Blackwell.

Masters, G. (1997a) 'Values for Probation, Society and Beyond', *Howard Journal of Criminal Justice*, 36, 3: 237–47.

Masters, G. (1997b) 'I Conflitti e la Mediazione Nelle Scuole in Giappone', in G. Pisapia and D Antonucci (eds.) *La Sfida della Mediazione*, Padova: CEDAM.

Masters, G. and Smith, D (1998) 'Portia and Persephone Revisited: Thinking about Feeling in Criminal Justice', *Theoretical Criminology*, 2, 1: 5–27.

Mayadas, N. S., Watts, T. D. and Elliott, D (eds.) (1997) International Handbook on Social Work Theory and Practice, London: Greenwood Press.

MacDonald, R. (1997a) 'Dangerous Youth and the Dangerous Class', in R. MacDonald (ed.), *Youth, the 'Underclass' and Social Exclusion*, London: Routledge.

MacDonald, R. (1997b) 'Youth, Social Exclusion and the Millennium', in R. MacDonald (ed.), *Youth, the 'Underclass' and Social Exclusion*, London: Routledge.

McGuire, J. (ed.) (1995) *What Works: Reducing Reoffending – Guidelines from Research and Practice*, Chichester: Wiley.

McNamara, J. (1996) 'Madness is a Feminist and a Disability Issue', in J. Morris (ed.), *Encounters With Strangers: Feminism and disability*, London: Women's Press.

McNulty, D (1997) 'Beyond a City's Limits', *The Herald*, 3 January.

Meekosha, H. and Dowse, L. (1997) 'Enabling Citizenship: Gender, Disability and Citizenship', *Feminist Review*, No 57.

Metz, E. (1997) 'Letter', *The Independent, Coordinator, UK Coalition Against Poverty*, 12 December.

Milne, K. (1998) *New Deal: Special Report* in New Statesman, 3 April.

Mouffe, C. (1993) *The Return of the Political*, London: Verso.

Moxon, D (1988) *Sentencing Practice in the Crown Court*, Home Office Research Study 103, London: HMSO.

Munday, B. and Ely, P. (eds.) (1996) Social Care in Europe, London: Prentice Hall/ Harvester Wheatsheaf.

Munn-Giddings, C. (1996) '*An Examination of the Self-help Movement in Relation to Feminist Theory, Citizenship and Democracy*'. Paper given at ISTR conference, Mexico City.

Murray, C. (1990) *The Emerging British Underclass,* London: Institute for Economic Affairs.

NACRO (unpublished) Race and Criminal Justice Unit Statistics, London: NACRO.

NASW (1973) *Standards for Social Service Manpower,* Washington DC: National Association of Social Workers.

Nellis, M. (1995) 'Towards a New View of Probation Values', In R. Hugman and D Smith (eds.) *Ethical Issues in Social Work,* London: Routledge.

NISW (1982) *Social Workers, their Role and Tasks,* London: National Institute for Social Work.

NISW (1996) *Social Exclusion, Civil Society and Social Work*, Briefing No. 18, London: National Institute for Social Work.

Normann, R. (1991) *Service Management,* Chichester: John Wiley and Sons.

Oldfield, A. (1990) *Citizenship and Community: Civic Republicanism and the Modern World,* London: Routledge.

Oliver, M. (1990) *The Politics Of Disablement,* Basingstoke: Macmillan.

Oliver, M. (1996) *Understanding Disability: From Theory to Practice,* Basingstoke: Macmillan.

Oliver, M. and Barnes, C. (1991) 'Discrimination, Disability and Welfare: from Needs to Rights' in I. Bynoe, M. Oliver and C. Barnes (eds.) *Equal Rights for Disabled People,* London: Institute for Public Policy Research.

ONS (1996) *Charities Assets: Survey of Charities*, London: Office of National Statistics.

Pahl, R. (1990*) 'Prophets, Ethnographers and Social Glue: Civil Society and Social Order',* Paper given at ESRC/CNRS Workshop on Citizenship, Social Order and Civilising Processes, Cumberland Lodge, September.

Parton, N (ed.) (1996) *Social Theory, Social Change and Social Work,* London: Routledge.

Pateman, C. (1989), *The Disorder of Women,* Cambridge: Polity Press.

People First (1994) *Outside, but not Inside ... Yet! Leaving Hospital and Living in the Community: an Evaluation by people with Learning Difficulties*, London: People First.

Peatfield, Z. (1998) 'Achievable Goals?' in Community Care, 26 February – 4 March.

Pepinsky, H. E. (1991) 'Peacemaking in Criminology and Criminal Justice', in H. E. Pepinsky and R. Quinney (eds.) *Criminology as Peacemaking,* Bloomington and Indianapolis: Indiana University Press.

Pepinsky, H. E. (1995) *A Peacemaking Primer* (http://www.soci.niu.edu~critcrim/ pepinsky/hal.primer).

Pepinsky, H. E. and Quinney, R. (eds.) (1991) *Criminology as Peacemaking*, Bloomington and Indianapolis: Indiana University Press.

Perske, R. (1991) *Unequal Justice?: What Can Happen when Persons with Retardation or Other Developmental Disabilities Encounter the Criminal Justice System,* Nashville, USA: Abingdon Press.

Peters, M. (1997) 'Social Exclusion' in Contemporary European Social Policy: Some Critical Comments' in G. Lavery, J. Pender and M. Peters (eds.) *'Exclusion and Inclusion': Minorities in Europe,* ISPRU Occasional Papers in Social Studies, Leeds: Leeds Metropolitan University.

Pincus, A. and Minahan, A. (1973) *Social Work Practice: Model and Method,* Ithaca, IU: F.E. Peacock.

Potts, M. and Fido, R. (1991) '*A Fit Person To Be Removed': Personal Accounts of Life in a Mental Deficiency Institution,* Plymouth: Northcote House.

Power, A. and Tunstall, R. (1997*) 'Dangerous Disorder: Riots and Violent Disturbances in Thirteen Areas of Britain'*, Findings 116, York: York Publishing Services, for the Joseph Rowntree Foundation.

Putnam, R. D (1993), 'The Prosperous Community: Social Capital and Public Life', *The American Prospect,* No 13.

Race, D (1995) 'Historical Development Of Service Provision', in N. Malin (ed.) *Services for People With Learning Disabilities*, London: Routledge.

Ranson, S. and Stewart, J. (1994) *Management for the Public Domain*, Basingstoke: Macmillan.

Raynor, P. (1991) 'Sentencing with and without reports', *Howard Journal of Criminal Justice*, 30, 4: 293–300.

Raynor, P. and Vanstone, M. (1996) 'Reasoning and Rehabilitation in Britain: the Results of the Straight Thinking on Probation (STOP) Programme', *International Journal of Offender Therapy and Comparative Criminology*, 40, 4: 272–84.

Raynor, P., Smith, D and Vanstone, M. (1994) *Effective Probation Practice*, Basingstoke: Macmillan.

Rex, S. (1997) *'Desistance from Offending: Experiences of Probation',* Paper to British Criminology Conference, Belfast, July.

Roberts, K. (1997) 'Is there an Emerging British 'Underclass'?' in R. MacDonald (ed.) *Youth, the 'Underclass' and Social Exclusion*, London: Routledge.

Rock, P. (1990) *Helping Victims of Crime: The Home Office and the Rise of Victim Support in England and Wales*, Oxford: Clarendon Press.

Room, G. (1994) 'Poverty Studies in the European Union: Retrospect and Prospect', Paper presented to the Conference 'Understanding Social Exclusion: Lessons from Transnational Research Studies', London, November.

Room, G. (ed.) (1995) *Beyond the Threshold: the Measurement and Analysis of Social Exclusion*, Bristol: The Policy Press.

Room, G. (1995) 'Poverty and Social Exclusion: The New European Agenda for Policy and Research' in G. Room (ed.), *Beyond the Threshold: the Measurement and Analysis of Social Exclusion*, Bristol: The Policy Press.

Rose, G. and Marshall, T. F. (1974) *Counselling and School Social Work*, London: John Wiley.

Rowntree, B. S. (1901) *Poverty: A Study of Town Life*, London: Macmillan.

Ryan, J. with Thomas, F. (1987) *The Politics Of Mental Handicap*, (Revised edition), London: Free Association Books.

Sako, M. (1992) *Prices Quality and Trust,* Cambridge: Cambridge University Press

Sanders, D S. and Pedersen, P. (1984) 'Introduction', in D. S. Sanders and P. Pedersen (eds.), *Education for International Social Welfare*, Honolulu: University of Hawaii.

Scottish Homes (1996) *The Physical Quality of Housing – Housing for Older People and Disabled People: A Consultation on Design Guidance,* Scottish Homes.

Scraton, P. and Chadwick, K. (1996) 'The Theoretical and Political Priorities of Critical Criminology' in J. Muncie, E. McLaughlin and M. Langan (eds.), *Criminological Perspectives*, London: Sage.

Seebohm Report (1968) *Report of the Committee on Local Authority and Allied Personal.*

Shardlow, S (ed.) (1989) The Values of Change in Social Work, London: Tavistock/ Routledge.

Shaw, C. (1994) *Changing Lives*, London: Policy Studies Institute.

Sheridan, A. (1980) *Michel Foucault: the Will to Truth*, London: Tavistock.

Silver, H. (1994) 'Social Exclusion and Social Solidarity: Three Paradigms' in *International Labour Review,* 133(5–6): 531–578.

142   *Social Exclusion*

Silver, H. and Wilkinson, F. (1995) 'Policies to Combat Social Exclusion: A French-British Comparison' in G. Rodgers, C. Gore and J. B. Figueiredo (eds.) *Social Exclusion: Rhetoric, Reality, Responses*, Geneva: IILS.
Sinclair, I & Gibbs, I. (1996) *Quality of Care in Children's Homes*, Working Paper Series B, No.3, University of York.
Sinfield, A. (1969) *Which Way for Social Work?* London: The Fabian Society.
Smith, D. (1995) *Criminology for Social Work*, Basingstoke: Macmillan.
Smith, D. and Stewart, J. (1997) 'Probation and Social Exclusion', *Social Policy and Administration*, 11, 5: 96–115.
Smith, D., Blagg, H. and Derricourt, N. (1988) 'Mediation in South Yorkshire', *British Journal of Criminology*, 28, 3, 378–395.
Smithers, R. and Milne, S. (1997) 'Labour: We do Want to End Poverty', *The Guardian,* August 15: 1.
Social Exclusion Unit, (1997) *Social Exclusion Unit,* Cabinet Office Homepage, http://www.open.gov.uk/co/seu/seu/home.htm, London, Cabinet Office, 5 December.
Specht, H. and Vickery, A. (eds.) (1977) *Integrating Social Work Methods,* London: George Allen and Unwin.
Spicker, P. (1997a) 'Exclusion and Citizenship in France', in M. Mullard (ed.) *The Politics of Social Policy,* London: Edward Elgar.
Spicker, P. (1997b) 'The Social Policy of the European Union', *Journal of Common Market Studies,* 35(i): 131–141.
Stalker, K. (1998) 'Some Ethical and Methodological Issues in Research with People with Learning Difficulties', *Disability and Society*, 13, 1: 5–19.
Stein, M. and Carey, K. (1986) *Leaving Care*, Oxford: Blackwell.
Steinberg, D L. (1997) *Bodies in Glass: Genetics, Eugenics, Embryo Ethics*, Manchester: Manchester University Press.
Stern, V. (1996) 'Let the Ex-cons Back in', *The Guardian*, 2 May: 15.
Stewart, G. and Stewart, J. (1993) *Social Circumstances of Younger Offenders under Probation Supervision*, Wakefield: ACOP.
Swann, M. (1985) *Education for All: the Report of the Committee of Inquiry into the Education of Children from Ethnic Minority Groups,* London: HMSO.
Taylor, D (1989) 'Citizenship and Social Policy', *Critical Social Policy*, 26: 19–31.
Taylor, P. (1995) Speech made to a joint NACRO/Leeds Race Issues Advisory Committee/ West Yorkshire Area Criminal Justice Liaison Committee Conference, Leeds, 30 June.
Thompson, N. (1993), *Anti-Discriminatory Practice,* Basingstoke: Macmillan.
Thomson, J. (1997) *The Everyday Lives of Service Users and Social Welfare Workers: a Materialist Analysis,* PhD, University of James Cook.
Thornton, P. and Tozer, R. (1995) *Having a Say in Change: Older People and Community Care*, York: Joseph Rowntree Foundation.
Tiemann, S. (1993) Opinion on Social Exclusion, *Official Journal of the European Union* OJ93/C 352/13.
Titterton, M. (1992) 'Managing Threats to Welfare: the Search for a New Paradigm of Welfare' *Journal of Social Policy,* vol. 21(1): 1–23.
Townsend, P. (1979) *Poverty in the United Kingdom*, London: Harmondsworth Penguin.
Townsend, P. (1993) *The International Analysis of Poverty*, Hemel Hempstead: Harvester Wheatsheaf.
Townsend, P. (1995) *The Rise of International Social Policy,* Bristol: The Policy Press.
Tredgold, A. F. (1909) 'The Feebleminded: A Social Danger', *Eugenics Review*, 1: 97–104.
Trinder, L. (1996) 'Social Work Research: the State of the Art (or Science)', *Child and Family Social Work*, 1, 233–242.

UK Coalition Against Poverty, Participation Sub-Group, (1997) *Poverty And Participation: Learnings from a September 1996 Workshop Bringing Together People Living in Poverty Throughout the UK*, London: UK Coalition Against Poverty.

Umbreit, M. and Roberts, A. (1996) *Mediation of Criminal Conflict in England: An Assessment of Services in Coventry and Leeds*, St. Paul, MN: Center for Restorative Justice and Mediation.

UNDP (1997) *Human Development Report 1997*, Oxford: Oxford University Press.

Vogel, U. (1988) 'Under Permanent Guardianship; Women's Condition Under Modern Civil Law', in B. Jones and A. G. Jónasdóttir (eds.) *The Political Interests of Gender*, London: Sage.

Walker, A. (1990) 'Blaming the Victims' in C. Murray (ed.) *The Emerging British Underclass*, London: Institute for Economic Affairs.

Walker, R.(1995) 'The Dynamics of Poverty and Social Exclusion' in G. Room (ed.) *Beyond the Threshold: the Measurement and Analysis of Social Exclusion*, Bristol: The Policy Press.

Walker, R. (1998) 'Poverty and Social Exclusion in Europe', in A. Walker and C. Walker (eds.) *Britain Divided: The Growth of Social Exclusion in the 1980s and 1990s*, London: Child Poverty Action Group.

Wann, M. (1995) *Building Social Capital. Self Help in a Twentieth Century Welfare State*, London: Institute of Public Policy Research.

Ward, H. (1995) *Looking After Children: Research into Practice*, London: HMSO.

Wardhaugh, J. and Wilding, P. (1993) 'Towards an Explanation of the Corruption of Care', *Critical Social Policy*, Issue 37: 4–31.

Waterhouse, L. (1997) 'Promoting Community Development', *Community Care*, 3–9 July.

Weale, A. (1991), 'Citizenship Beyond Borders' In U. Vogel and M. Moran (eds.) *The Frontiers of Citizenship*, Basingstoke: Macmillan.

Weeks, J. (1993) 'Rediscovering Values', in J. Squires (ed.) *Principled Positions*, London: Lawrence & Wishart.

Weeks, J. (1996) 'The Idea of a Sexual Community', *Soundings*, 2: 71–84.

Weiss, C. (1995) 'Nothing as Practical as Good Theory: Exploring Theory-based Evaluation', in J. Connell, A. Kuboch, L. Schon and C. Weiss (eds.) *New Approaches to Evaluating Community Initiatives: Concepts, Methods and Contexts*, Washington DC: The Aspen Institute.

White, V. (1996) *Paying Attention to People*, London: SPCK.

Wilkinson, R. (1998) 'What Health Tells Us About Society' in A. de Haan and S. Maxwell (eds.) *Poverty and Social Exclusion in North and South*, Vol. 29, No. 1, January, IDS Bulletin: 10–19.

Williams, F. (1992) 'Somewhere Over the Rainbow: Universality and Diversity in Social Policy', in N. Manning and R. Page (eds.) *Social Policy Review 4*, Canterbury: Social Policy Association.

Williams, F. (1996) 'Feminism, Postmodernism and the Question of Difference', in N. Parton (ed.) *Social Work, Social Theory and Social Change*, London: Routledge

Williams, F. and Popay, J. (in press) 'Balancing Polarities: Developing a New Framework for Welfare Research', in F. Williams, J. Popay, and A. Oakley, *Welfare Research: A Critical review and New Synthesis*, London: UCL Press.

Williams, F., Popay , J. and Oakley, A. (in press) *Welfare Research: A Critical review and New Synthesis*, London: UCL Press.

Wilmott, P. and Young, M. (1957) *Family and Kinship in East London*, London: Routledge & Kegan Paul.

Wilson, G. (1994) 'Co-production and Self Care: New Approaches to Managing Community Care Services for Older People', *Social Policy and Administration*, 26, 3: 236–250.

Wilson, G. (ed.) (1995) *Community Care: Asking the Users*, London: Chapman and Hall.

Wilson, J. (1996) 'Self Service', *Community Care*, 15–21 February.

Wistow, G., Knapp, M., Hardy, B., Forder, J., Kendall, I. and Manning, R. (1996) *Social Care Markets: Progress and Prospects*, Buckingham: Open University Press.

Wolfensberger, W. and Tullman, S. (1990) 'A Brief Outline of the Principle of Normalisation', in A. Bachin and J. Walmsley (eds.) *Making Connections: Reflecting on the Lives and Experiences of People with Hearing Disabilities*, Sevenoaks: Hodder & Stoughton.

Wolfensberger, W. (1992) *The New Genocide of Handicapped and Afflicted People*, Revised edition, Syracuse, NY.

Wolfensberger, W. (1994) 'The Growing Threat to the Lives of Handicapped People in the Context of Modernistic Values', *Disability and Society*, Vol. 9, No 3, 395–413.

The World Bank (1994) *The World Bank and Participation*, Washington DC: The World Bank.

Yeatman, A. (1993) 'Voice and Representation in the Politics of Difference' in Gunew, S. and Yeatman, A. (eds.), *Feminism and the Politics of Difference*, Australia, Allen and Unwin.

Yeatman, A. (1994) *Post-modern Revisionings of the Political*, London: Routledge.

Young, I. M. (1989) 'Polity and Group Difference: a Critique of the Ideal of Universal Citizenship', *Ethics*, 99: 250–74.

Young, I. M. (1990) *Justice and the Politics of Difference*, Oxford: Princeton University Press.

Young, I. M. (1993) 'Together in Difference: Transforming the Logic of Group Political Conflict' in J. Squires (ed.) *Principled Positions*, London: Lawrence & Wishart.

Yuval-Davis, N. (1997) *Gender and Nation*, London: Sage.

Index

KING ALFRED'S COLLEGE